Absolutely Positively
CONNECTICUT

Diane Smith

The
Globe
Pequot
press

Guilford, Connecticut

Paul and Caroline,
To lead you
on many
new adventures
that are
positively
Connecticut!
diane smith
12·5·00
CT Creative Store

Cover photo © Jack McConnell
Back cover photo © Julie Bidwell
Cover design by Saralyn Twomey
Text design by Libby Kingsbury
Photo credits:
CPTV video stills pp 2–6, 24–26, 50–54, 58–59, 95–96, 98–101, 114–16, 130–32, 136–41, 148–53. Photographers: Kevin Kuhl, Michael Dunphy, Vic Vincze, Phil Candito, Chris Simmons, Joe Fox. All other video stills from WTNH-TV 8. Photographers: Ken Melech, John Roll, Kort Frydenborg, Mark Ciesinski, Tim Clune, Mark Desy, George DeYounge, Tom Parent, Joe Sferrazza, RJ Tattersall, Tim Wright, Pat Child.
Many thanks to the following people and organizations for providing supplemental photographs: pp i, 97 Mystic Whaler Cruises; pp i, 151, 153 Charles R. Morrissey; pp iii, 4–6 Yale University Photographer Michael Marsland and The Sterling Memorial Library, Manuscripts and Archives, Yale University; pp iii, 27, 29 Railroad Museum of New England/Naugatuck Railroad Company; pp iii, 63 Desserts by David Glass; pp iv, 75 Howard Shapiro; pp iv, 107 National Park Service, Weir Farm National Historic Site; pp iv, 117, 118 Suzanne Sankow; pp iv, 143 Claudia Boerst; pp v, 154 © Phillip Fortune/Connecticut Public Television & Radio; pp1, 17 Father Tom Poth; p3 Northeast Connecticut Visitors District; p9 Barker Character, Comic and Cartoon Museum; p10 Gladys and Richard Mann; p13 Vivian Perlis; p20 Peters Railroad Museum; p23 Dale Carson; pp24–26 Ballard Institute and Museum of Puppetry; p31 Cato Corner Farm; p35 The Barnum Museum; p37 © Amy Wilton; p38 Stew Leonard's; pp40–41 The Witch Hazel Works; p43 Pez Candy, Inc.; p44 Sunrise Herb Farm; p45 Martha's Herbary; p47 courtesy Stony Creek Quarry Celebration; p49 Libby Kingsbury; pp51–52 Sharpe Hill Vineyard; p55 Harney & Sons Fine Tea; pp56–57 Susan Flavin; p58 Farmington Valley Visitors Association; pp 64–65 Paula Brisco; p69 Barbara and Seldon Wells; p70 Buster Scranton; p71, 87 The National Theatre of the Deaf; p72 © Peter Tytla; p76 Gilchrist Publishing; p79 Zuckermann Harpsichords International; p81 Sewtique; p82 Cheryl and Scott McNeal; p85 Synia and Jeff McQuillan; p90–92 Hill-Stead Museum; pp93, 99 Sunbeam Fleet; pp94–95 © Mystic Seaport, Mystic Connecticut. All rights reserved; p103 Bill Murray/Center Church; p105 Toshi Otsuki, courtesy Victoria magazine; p108 B.F. Clyde's Cider Mill; p111 The Dudley Foundation; p113 John Motley; p115 Janet L. Serra; p120 Constance Bombaci; pp122–23 Thomas and Ann Cummings; p124 Eileen McCaughern; p125 Marcia Herman; p126 Kristin Elliott Leas; p129 © Les Burdge; p132 The Fidelco Guide Dog Foundation; p133 Bonnie Jennings Steele, Stamford Hospital; p134 Shelley Wolf; p135 Harkness Memorial State Park; p140 Naval Submarine Base New London; p145 Travis Ford; p147 Robert Conrad Ledoux; p150 Gillette Castle State Park.

Library of Congress Cataloging-in-Publication Data is available.
ISBN 0-7627-0847-6 (hardcover) 0-7627-0810-7 (pbk.)

Manufactured in Canada
First Edition/First Printing

CONTENTS

PREFACE

As a news anchor and reporter, I've heard time and again that people feel there's nothing but bad news on TV. So I set out to discover the good news, the stories that make people feel good about living in Connecticut. That's how the *Positively Connecticut* news segment started on WTNH-TV 8 more than fifteen years ago.

Positively Connecticut found a new home in 1999 with the only TV station that has Connecticut as its first name, Connecticut Public Television (CPTV). These days, as I roam the highways and byways of this wonderful state, preparing my television broadcasts, I am now able to tell the stories that are positively Connecticut in an expanded form. There is more time to let the stories breathe and let the characters who make our state special reveal themselves.

The stories are about the people and places that make our corner of New England great; that give it character and heart and tradition. My first book, *Positively Connecticut,* was a collection of some of my favorite stories. They seem to have struck a chord, because so many of you asked for a sequel. Here it is!

The stories in *Absolutely Positively Connecticut* first came alive on television thanks to gifted videographers from both Channel 8 and CPTV. Their images have been captured to illustrate these stories. We have enhanced this book with additional photographs, many of them from the subjects' own collections. Some of the stories first appeared on the air more than a dozen years ago, some very recently. All have been updated to tell you "the rest of the story."

I hope this book will reinforce your feeling that Connecticut is a great place to live and work, and I encourage you to seek your own adventures that are absolutely positively Connecticut.

I'll see you on CPTV!

ACKNOWLEDGMENTS

To the cast of characters who are absolutely positively Connecticut, thanks for sharing your passions with us. Thanks to the viewers who tune in to see more good news about Connecticut.

Thanks to Arthur Diedrick, the President and Chairman of the Connecticut Development Authority, for ensuring that *Positively Connecticut* continues. Thank you to CPTV for embracing *Positively Connecticut,* and to Jerry Franklin for his vision. Larry Rifkin, you have made CPTV the place for telling the stories of Connecticut. Thanks to Haig Papasian and Bette Blackwell for making magic happen on each program.

Gifted photographers have brought these stories to life, especially Ken Melech, who made every day on the road an adventure. To John Roll, thanks for being my partner through hundreds of shoots and thousands of miles on the highways and byways of Connecticut. It is a pleasure to find the words that enhance the pictures taken by the videographers of CPTV and WTNH.

I am grateful to Michele Russo, a wonderful producer and a steadfast friend.

Thanks to my mentor, Kenn Venit, who helped me find the path. Roxanne Coady of R. J. Julia Booksellers and Faith Middleton of Connecticut Public Radio, thanks for your belief in the literary value of *Positively Connecticut.*

Thanks to the team at The Globe Pequot Press, including Linda Kennedy, Mike Urban, Kevin Lynch, Saralyn D'Amato-Twomey, Dana Baylor, Melodie Goldstein, Lisa Reneson, and Libby Kingsbury. Thanks to Paula Brisco, an editor who makes every story better, and to Jane Reilly for unflagging support and enthusiasm.

Mom, thanks for teaching me the first draft is never the last, and Dad, thanks for showing me that each person has a story to tell if you are patient enough to listen. To my sisters and brother and their spouses, thanks for listening. You are everything a family should be.

To my husband, Tom Woodruff, whose love makes all things possible, there are not enough ways to say thank you.

This book is dedicated to Max Showalter, from Kansas via Hollywood, whose heart was absolutely positively Connecticut.

Dreamers and Doers

BACK IN BUSINESS

I t was a town that many businesses had abandoned, but potential is what one man saw when he moved from California to Connecticut's Quiet Corner.

The Putnam of today with its bustling streets and busy shops is a far cry from the Putnam Jerry Cohen first saw nine years ago.

Jerry: "It looked like everybody was getting out as fast as they could, or they had already gotten out. It didn't look very inviting. There were lots of For Rent signs."

But Jerry fell in love with a vacant department store.

Jerry: "As an antiques dealer for the last twenty-five years, I have grown attached to the Victorian period of architecture. Coming into Putnam, there was this huge old building for sale, with pressed-tin ceilings and hardwood maple floors, and it just was totally appealing to me."

Jerry decided to convert the store into a market-place, where hundreds of antiques dealers could rent space. Everyone warned him against it.

Jerry: "Everybody—the real estate agents, the bankers, the people in town. Putnam was seen as a town that was past its prime, on a downhill slide, that would never recover, that would always be a terrible place to do business."

But instead of being discouraged by the naysayers, Jerry was even more motivated.

Jerry: "I had a vision, and I was able to enlist enough people in taking on a piece of that vision, and seeing it the way I saw it, that we were able to create something in Putnam that everybody could be proud of—that would be good for town and people who come into town."

One of the people he enlisted was Mayor Daniel Rovero.

Rovero: "My motto's been that everybody who comes to town is a customer. It wasn't a case of us giving him free taxes and all sorts of incentives and so forth, it was just hard work and friendship."

It took four years for the business to get into the black, but Jerry has attracted hundreds of dealers to his marketplace, where they sell everything from high-end Stickley furniture, Jerry's specialty, to jewelry, tableware, and almost any collectible you can imagine.

Jerry: "We do have some shoppers who come in here at ten in the morning, and at five in the afternoon they are still here and kind of bleary-eyed."

Cheryl Smith and Madeline Barry drove in from Massachusetts to shop.

Cheryl: "We've been enjoying it so far. It's been terrific. There's lots more than we can possibly see in one afternoon."

Diane: "Buying anything?"

Madeline: "Yeah, we're working on it. We can't get out of this place because we're looking into every case and at every item. We're having fun!"

The success of the Antiques Marketplace drew other antiques dealers to town. Now there are about 450 of them within 100 feet, and lots of other businesses, too, including restaurants and crafts shops and framing stores.

Bob Rubenoff began by renting space in the Antiques Marketplace but later opened his own store, which specializes in architectural antiques.

Bob: "I took about 352 buildings down by hand, myself, and I put a lot of what I salvaged into storage. Then I bought this building about five years ago. I always

wanted to have a really nice store so I created this out of the parts and pieces of the mansions that I took apart."

Lisa Cassettari grew up nearby. She never considered opening a business in Putnam until the Antiques Marketplace started a turnaround in the business center. Now she runs the highly regarded Vine Bistro just down the block.

Lisa: "Myself and my business partner, we sat outside and counted people and cars and thought, 'OK, if a certain percentage of these people eat here, you know, we might make it.' After looking at the town for a long time, about three months, we said this is a really smart decision."

There are lots of shoppers and browsers in town. Jerry thinks there are two main reasons for Putnam's success. Shoppers like the convenience of parking once and finding multiple shops all within an easy walk. And because rent and overhead are not very high in Putnam, shoppers can find some bargains. The majority of items sell for under $100, although some high-end dealers are moving into town, too.

Bob Rubenoff welcomes them all.

Bob: "There are so many antiques dealers in this town that it has created a frenzy in the antiques world. People come from all over to see Putnam and see what Putnam has to offer. The crime rate is very low. I just think it's a great little town."

Mayor Rovero says that the vitality downtown is spreading. The old mills, long abandoned by thread and button companies, are reopening for office space and light industrial use.

Rovero: "We've had some difficult times. We had major fires and a flood that wiped out 35 percent of Putnam. But every time we have a disaster, we come back stronger. Like they say, you keep on smiling, tomorrow's another day. So I say, 'Let's see what we can do for tomorrow.'"

For an old mill town on the way back, Putnam's tomorrow looks positively Connecticut. ■

$\mathscr{M}$ORE:

The thriving downtown shopping area has helped encourage other businesses to move into town. Five of the old mills are now open again, humming with light manufacturing and office workers. ▫

MONUMENTAL ACHIEVEMENT

O ne of the newer tombstones at Evergreen Cemetery marks the grave of a man who died more than eighty years ago. Why did it take so long to mark his grave? It's a story that is positively Connecticut.

It's a lovely fall morning at New Haven's Evergreen cemetery, where 300 people are gathered. Members of Shades, a Yale University a cappella group, are standing beneath a tree, swaying slightly and softly singing. Dr. Curtis Patton is standing by a new headstone that reads: 1852–1918 EDWARD ALEXANDER BOUCHET.

Curtis Patton first learned about Edward Bouchet in 1952, as a student at Fisk University. He'd fallen asleep in a math class.

Curtis: *"The professor wanted to impress upon me the opportunity I was being given as a young black man to attain a college degree. He stopped the lecture and told the story of Bouchet. In fact, he said, staring at me, 'One hundred years ago there was a boy named Edward Bouchet of New Haven, Connecticut.'"*

A boy who rose above all obstacles to become the first African-American graduate of Yale. Curtis was inspired by the young man's determination, and

he never forgot the story of Edward Bouchet. Nearly twenty years later, in 1970, when Dr. Patton arrived at Yale as a newly hired professor of public health, he headed straight to the university archives to look him up.

Curtis: *"In those days they were still letting you see who had checked out what book, and there at the very top of the list was my old professor from Fisk, Lee Lorch."*

Edward Bouchet's story was truly remarkable:

Curtis: *"It really begins with his father, William, I think, who was a slave in*

*Charleston, whose chance it was and whose opportunity it was
to come to Yale as a servant to a student."*

Yale's chief research archivist, Judy Schiff, has found
mementos of that student, John Robertson. Sifting through
photos and class records and pictures, she learned that
when Robertson graduated from Yale, he emancipated
William Bouchet. William remained in New Haven,
working as a porter at Yale. The man who had arrived
in New Haven a slave was determined to send his son
Edward to Hopkins, the illustrious local private school.

Curtis Patton says that was an opportunity and a challenge for young Edward.

Curtis: *"His parents didn't look like others, and didn't have
the money the other parents had. It suggests to me that this boy
who went to Hopkins was a boy of great courage."*

Edward graduated from Hopkins as class valedictorian. He went on to study at
Yale, distinguishing himself in his studies, becom-
ing Yale's first black graduate in 1874, and later,
the first African-American to earn a Ph.D. In fact,
he was the sixth person of any race in the entire
Western Hemisphere to earn a Ph.D. in physics.

Curtis: *"In order for that to happen, somebody
had to say yes. Somebody had to affirm, to say
to Bouchet, 'You're OK, and what you're doing is
OK.'"*

But not everyone said yes to Bouchet. In spite
of his credentials, the upper echelon of science
was still not open to a black scholar. So Edward
Bouchet devoted twenty-six years of his life to teaching young African-Americans at
the School for Colored Youth in Philadelphia and at other institutions. In 1914 poor
health sent him home to New Haven to live with his aged mother and his sisters. Four
years later he died and was buried at Evergreen Cemetery.

A couple of years ago a trustee of the cemetery, Paul McCraven, told Curtis Patton that he'd
found Bouchet's grave and that it had no marker.

Curtis: *"I presume that it cost money and there-
fore was a kind of luxury that the family may not
have been able to afford."*

Curtis called on friends from town and gown
to right that wrong, and on a fine sunny October
morning they watch as a shiny black granite
headstone is unveiled in memory of Edward
Bouchet.

The memories of Bouchet are his legacy, and they have inspired James Anderson, a Hopkins student who speaks at the memorial.

James: *"I remember thinking how it must have been for him 100 years ago. In the face of oppression he continued to pursue his dream. So it encouraged me that no matter what's opposing me, I can achieve my dream."*

At the end of the service, Curtis Patton notes to himself that it has been a day for parts of the New Haven community to come together and say yes again to Bouchet.

Yes to a scholar and role model who was positively Connecticut. ■

*M*ORE:

A portrait of Edward Bouchet now hangs in Sterling Memorial Library on the Yale campus, an inspiration to students of all races. Dr. Curtis Patton is researching Bouchet's life for a book about him and other African-American pioneers. ■

A PASSION FOR ANIMATION

W hat do you call a man who likes to tell people he's six days younger than Popeye? A cartoon nut? A kid at heart? Both describe Herb Barker, who's passionate about animation.

Herb likes to share his joy with others, which is why he opened the Barker Character, Comic and Cartoon Museum in 1996.

Herb: *"Life's been good to us, and business has been good to us, and this is something my wife and I want to do."*

There's no charge to see his incredible collection, now overflowing from a formerly abandoned building in the backyard of his Cheshire business, Barker Specialties. The idea was Gloria's, Herb's partner in life, in business, and in collecting.

Gloria: *"I said, 'Well, let's have a museum, and then we can get all our toys in here,' thinking to myself, 'What a good way to get everything out of the house and the offices.'"*

"Everything" includes some 70,000 artifacts based on cartoon and comic strip characters, some dating back as much as 125 years. They range from a century-old gum dispenser based on the very first cartoon character known in this country, the Yellow Kid, to the Flintstones, to early Mickey Mouse collectibles, including a watch made in Waterbury and silver Mickey spoons and cups.

Herb: *"Because we're located right next to Meriden, we've been searching to find some of the character items that were made by International Silver, a company that used to be located there."*

Decades of searching have taken the Barkers to hundreds of sales, flea markets, and auctions. Once Herb spent six hours during a live auction on the telephone bidding on some old buttons.

Herb: *"I heard him say, 'The man from Connecticut wants a bathroom break,' and I heard everyone else say, 'Give it to him, give it to him,' so he said, 'You have three minutes.'"*

Claudia DiDato, the museum director, says the toughest part of her job is trying to find space in a museum that's already chock-full.

Diane: *"You have how many cases of other things you'd like to fit in?"*

Claudia: *"Lots and lots—enough to fill another museum right now."*

The Barker museum is a four-acre complex of fun. The "cartoon-scaped" grounds feature panoramas with larger-than-life-size characters from cartoons and old movies brought to life by soundtracks blaring from loudspeakers hidden in the trees.

An old stable located on the property has been converted into a cartoon theater, and there's a large animation gallery, too, selling cartoon cels and collectibles, and offering drawing classes and workshops for kids. But the heart of the place is in the Barkers' personal collection.

Claudia: *"The Barkers and all of us that work here enjoy seeing the faces on everyone who just walks through the door and goes 'Oh my goodness!'"*

You might imagine that Herb Barker's love of comics developed in childhood. Not so.

Herb: *"My father had a family food store, and I didn't have a chance to see many movies because I was working in the store all the time. So I grew up without these characters. Maybe that's what I'm doing now, reliving the childhood I never had."*

Now Herb helps others relive their childhood memories in a way that's positively Connecticut. ∎

*𝒮*INCE OUR STORY:

The Barkers bought all the original artwork used in the filming of the Gumby *TV series, as well as an extensive collection of California Raisin animation sets, props, and artwork used in filming the award-winning commercials and television specials. Now plans are in the works to expand to make room for a California Raisin and Gumby Museum.*

The Barkers have donated fifty pieces of artwork called cels—the animation frames of cartoons—to MidState Medical Center in Meriden. The donated collection is valued at $60,000.

In 1999 Animation *magazine named the Barkers among the ten most influential people in the industry.* ∎

BABY BOOM

T*here's a population explosion in Old Saybrook at the Mann house. The family has grown so large, they've added an addition—a dollhouse, they call it. It's home to thousands and thousands and thousands of dolls.*

For Gladys Mann, collecting dolls all began innocently enough.

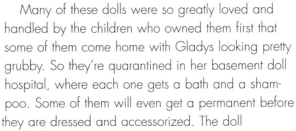

Gladys: *"I started when my daughter was going away to college in 1978. We went to tag sales looking for things for her to take to college, and then I found a few old dirty dolls and brought them home and cleaned them up."*

Many of these dolls were so greatly loved and handled by the children who owned them first that some of them come home with Gladys looking pretty grubby. So they're quarantined in her basement doll hospital, where each one gets a bath and a shampoo. Some of them will even get a permanent before they are dressed and accessorized. The doll wardrobe fills several bureaus, and the clothes are so nice that Gladys loans some of them to real babies to wear for a while.

Only after the dolls are brought back to nearly new condition do they find a place in the collection. They are lovingly lined up on shelves that run the entire length and width of the room, shoulder to shoulder. The army of dolls fills every space except for narrow pathways to admire them from.

Gladys: *"I'm gonna have to think of some way to get a little more*

room because my husband has already told me I can't have his garage."

But husband Richard doesn't object when the dolls keep coming home. He says collecting and caring for the dolls helped Gladys get through several cancer surgeries, and they not

only bring joy to Gladys, but also to people who visit.

Richard: *"It brings back a lot of memories, a lot of memories. They come in here and start walking down memory lane. They'll*
say, *'Oh, I remember this when I was a child, I remember that when I was a kid.'*

That's what happened when I spotted Charmin' Chatty, the first talking doll I ever had! I still remember the Christmas morning I found her under the tree.

There are something like fourteen thousand dolls in one room. That's a lot of memories and a lot of nostalgia—and, you might think, a lot of dusting. Except the Manns have figured that all out. No, they don't come through here with a feather duster; they don't have to.

Richard installed a state-of-the-art electronic air cleaner.

Richard: *"As the air returns, the dirt gets flipped up to the electric things down there in the furnace, and it burns the dust away and then it comes back up clean again."*

It's a home fit for a queen. The Queen Elizabeth I doll resides right next to the Duke, John Wayne, in a cavalry costume, and the King (of Pop, that is), Michael Jackson. Jacko's flanked by Marilyn Monroe, Little Orphan Annie, and Pee-Wee Herman, and more celebrities than there are in Hollywood.

Diane: *"Do you ever say to yourself, okay this is enough, fourteen thousand is enough?"*

Gladys: *"I have said that and then sort of thought, 'Wait a minute, I don't have that one.'"*

It seems there's always one more doll that needs a home, a home that's positively Connecticut. ∎

Gladys Mann's collection now numbers fifteen thousand dolls "at least," she says. They've spilled out of the special addition and into the basement, which Richard has renovated for them. Gladys is still scouring tag sales, searching for other orphans in need of love. She doesn't often attend doll shows, though, saying, "It's not a challenge to pay full price."

The collection is not open to the public, but the Manns have had lots visitors referred by people they know. Gladys has seen small children beg their grandmothers to "buy me that one," but she never sells a doll. Recently, though, Richard says they've started to talk about eventually selling the entire collection to a single buyer. It may take a while to find the right customer—the collection has an appraised value of more than one million dollars. ▪

TALKING MUSIC

D uke Ellington, Leonard Bernstein, John Cage, Aaron Copland—the composers who shaped American music in this century—have all talked with a Weston woman who is the Barbara Walters of the music world. But Vivian Perlis doesn't conduct her interviews just for today. They're for posterity.

From the basement of Stoeckel Hall at Yale University, the sounds of the greats in American music—and the sometimes surprising details of their lives—are cataloged in more than 900 taped interviews.

From the composer of "Appalachian Spring," Aaron Copland, comes the revelation that he didn't get much encouragement in music early in his life.

Voice of Aaron Copland: *"My father said, 'We spent a lot of money on lessons for the older kids, and not much came of it, so why would I spend any more money on you?'"*

That's the kind of precious tidbit that Vivian Perlis has gathered in thirty years of recording the oral history of twentieth-century American music.

Vivian started interviewing composers, and those who knew them best, almost by accident. In 1969, while a reference librarian at the Yale School of Music, she happened to meet a life-long friend of the composer Charles Ives, who lived much of his life in Connecticut.

Vivian: *"I thought it would be interesting to get something in his own voice. I didn't even know that the act I was about to commit is called oral history."*

Continuing to record music history from the people who made it took dogged determination. Vivian had to find funding and overcome the skeptics.

Vivian: *"The Yale librarian at that time was very open about the fact that only written materials should be library materials."*

But Vivian persisted. In interviews with everyone from ragtime's Eubie Blake, to jazz giant Duke Ellington, to the master of the avant-garde John Cage, Vivian gives us a look at the people behind the music, sometimes filling in the gaps in the written history. She wisely started with the oldest and most fragile of these important figures, but she has also spotlighted young composers, whom she revisits at five-year intervals.

Vivian: *"It's about the early years, it's the childhood years, the maturing years, the influences, both musical and otherwise."*

And Vivian has a way with interviews. The first time she met with Leonard Bernstein at his home in Fairfield County, they'd planned a one-hour session. Bernstein ended up talking to Vivian for more than six hours.

Along the way Vivian has written several award-winning books and produced three documentaries. And as you might expect, after spending more than thirty years compiling the oral history of the music of the last one hundred years, Vivian plans to commemorate the century.

Vivian: *"It will be a book with CDs of the history of American music in the twentieth century, as told by its creative figures."*

Talking music with Vivian Perlis. She's creating an oral history treasure that is positively Connecticut. ∎

*M*ORE:

In 2000 music lovers celebrated the centennial of Aaron Copland's birth, and many sought out Vivian Perlis for insight into his genius.

Aaron Copland said many times that he always intended to write an autobiography, but never would have gotten it done without Vivian. When Copland was awarded the Congressional Gold Medal in 1986, he was too frail to attend the ceremony. He asked Vivian to stand in for him. ∎

ANGIE'S KIDS

Most folks in New Milford know Angie Santana. Some stopped by her candy shop, Sweet Blooms, near town hall to buy her handmade chocolates. Many knew Angie as their kids' school bus driver, a job she held for twelve years. That may tell you about Angie's measure of patience and her love for kids, a love that extended beyond her own six children to the three boys whose mother had been her childhood friend.

Angie and Chrystine had been schoolgirls together in Scotland, but when Angie came to America in 1964, she lost track of Chrystine—until 1979 when she heard that Chrystine and her twin sister, Isobel, wanted to come to America, too. Angie put them up on her pullout couch until they got on their feet. A dozen years later, Chrystine needed that couch again.

By that time she was the mother of three little boys, she was in a bad marriage, and she was suffering from advanced breast cancer.

Angie: *"I picked her and the boys up, and kept them forever more."*

They moved into Angie's already crowded two-bedroom place. But although there may not have been much room in the house, Angie had plenty of room in her heart for her dying friend and her sons.

Angie: *"Chrystine's last will and testament says that she did not want the boys to be forced to return to their father."*

So Angie adopted the boys. And though their mom is gone, they keep her spirit and memory alive by raising money for breast cancer research. They make chocolate lollipops in the shape of remembrance ribbons and take them to local businesses, which sell them for a quarter apiece. At Linda Heslin's shop, Bodyworks, the lollipops sell briskly. Linda says making and selling the pops means more to the boys than just raising money to fight breast cancer.

Linda: *"They need to keep their mother's memory alive. It's healthy. Living with Angie helps them remember her."*

The kids raised $1,000 last year to fight breast cancer, the disease that claimed not just their mother,

*S*INCE OUR STORY:

Angie's kids reached their goal of raising $3,000, which they donated to Making Strides Against Breast Cancer, an annual fund-raiser organized by the American Cancer Society.

Angie closed her shop to take a full-time job with benefits, but she still makes candy for customers as far away as Tokyo. ■

but their grandmother and other relatives before her.

Angie: *"Maybe some day these guys will have daughters, too. The disease is in its third generation for this family, and there's no way that you cannot do something. You have to help."*

The boys have set a goal of raising $3,000 this year.

Angie: *"They're going to have a cure. I have no doubt whatsoever. I am going to feel proud that we were a part of it, and they will, too!"*

Angie's kids, part of a fight that's positively Connecticut. ■

LOOKING FORWARD
New Haven

Looking forward to the rest of your life. That's what Ellen Swirsky wants women with cancer to do. Ellen battled breast cancer right after the birth of her third child, and she decided cancer is a "temporary detour" that can be managed with the right information, treatment, and support. Ellen began a program called Looking Forward at the Hospital of Saint Raphael that offers everything from tips on nutrition to makeovers for looking and feeling your best during treatment. The education and wellness program has helped thousands of patients since 1993. For more information call (203) 789-3488. ■

THE SHRINE

W hen you think of a religious pilgrimage, you may think of Mecca or Jerusalem. But a shrine in Connecticut attracts the faithful, too.

In the Litchfield Hills there is a church without walls, and without a roof, unless you count the canopy of trees that overhangs the simple wooden benches at Lourdes of Litchfield. Some 30,000

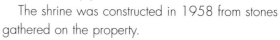

faithful flock here each year to pray at a stone grotto reminiscent of the one in Lourdes, France, where the Virgin Mary is said to have appeared to a girl named Bernadette. Father Eugene Lynch was a seminarian here, before the Montfort Missionaries built the shrine.

Father Lynch: *"This was just a little rock ledge where we students used to come with our books and sit on the rocks and study. There was a little stream babbling on the side. That's one of the memories I carried for forty years before I came back here."*

The shrine was constructed in 1958 from stones gathered on the property.

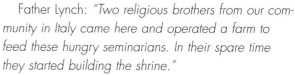

Father Lynch: *"Two religious brothers from our community in Italy came here and operated a farm to feed these hungry seminarians. In their spare time they started building the shrine."*

Today chipmunks scamper across the grotto as the three resident priests celebrate Mass or anoint the sick.

Father Lynch: *"They bring their cares and their concerns. They pray with Mary, and they ask the Lord to hear their prayers and help them in their difficulties as they carry their own personal crosses."*

Colette Boyd lives nearby in Litchfield.

Colette: *"You feel like you're with God and you're in His creation. There is a beautiful service that goes on here in praise of our Creator. It's just a very awesome experience."*

16

ABSOLUTELY POSITIVELY CONNECTICUT

Some come for religious retreats or to wander through the 160 acres. Others walk the quarter-mile along the Stations of the Cross—bronze figures that portray the sufferings and death of Christ.

Father Lynch: *"One of the favorite songs here is 'This Is Holy Ground.' Hopefully all ground is holy, but there are certain places where God seems to be a little bit more evident. This is one of those places."*

Ralph Rubino treasures his time here and drives up frequently from his home on the shoreline.

Ralph: *"When I am here, all the aesthetics of the world are right here. . ."*—he thumps his chest, over his heart—*"and it hits me right here."*

In 1998 the shrine was forty years old and beginning to show its age, as well as wear and tear from the weather. Volunteers mounted a campaign to raise $100,000 for its restoration.

Donna Valente visits often from Morris.

Donna: *"This place has always been very special. It's a feeling of peace and an almost overwhelming feeling of beauty."*

Lourdes of Litchfield . . . a place of peace that's positively Connecticut. ■

 FINAL WORD:

Restoration of the shrine is nearly complete. Father Tom Poth of the Montfort community calls Lourdes of Litchfield "the church with no doors." The property is open dawn to dusk year-round, and Mass is offered six days a week from May through mid-October at 11:30 A.M. Group pilgrimages can be arranged by contacting the shrine director in advance. For more information call (860) 567–1041. ■

MAKING WAVES

E ver feel like you hear the same songs on the radio over and over again? Not if you tune in to WPKN 89.5 FM. The station started in 1963, broadcasting into the dormitories at the University of Bridgeport. Today WPKN is a 10,000-watt FM station heard in many parts of the state and around the world on the Internet. It is one of the few stations in the country that depends entirely on listeners for financial support.

By day Richard Epstein is a dentist. At night he plays bassoon in the Norwalk Symphony. But on Wednesday, when his dental office is closed, he does an eclectic show on WPKN radio.

Richard: *"I play Bach, I play some avant-garde music, I play some music from the 1500s. I've played some Ani DiFranco, some storytelling by Utah Phillips. I have a very wide range in taste."*

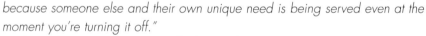

Other radio stations try to get you to tune in, but Harry Minot, the station manager, says WPKN is not afraid to tell listeners to tune out.

Harry: *"I always explain to the brand-new listener that there are times when you will have to turn the thing off. Never feel bad when that happens, because someone else and their own unique need is being served even at the moment you're turning it off."*

The radio station boasts a staff of eighty-five unpaid, part-time programmers, or on-air personalities, who have complete freedom in choosing what to air. The only things off limits: using words banned by the FCC, or being conventional.

Some songs I like.

Some songs I don't like

Programmers bring in their own selections or choose from the offerings in an extraordinary music library of some 40,000 CDs and 40,000 LPs. Each CD and LP is categorized by the date of its arrival at the station. Holding the number one position: an album by Judy Garland recorded in 1963.

Bumper stickers distributed by the station read "WPKN: Some songs I like, some

songs I don't like." That's no surprise, since programmers play everything from bebop, to Brazilian music, to bluegrass, and beyond—way beyond.

Renowned bass player Phil Bowler's show airs jazz of every stripe.

Phil: *"My idea when I volunteered here fifteen years ago was to give something back to the community. I felt that many of the disc jockeys on commercial stations were giving wrong information out about the musicians and not giving enough information for listeners."*

The staff fondly describes those listeners as "thinkers, dreamers, cranks, and misfits." They are also the only source of funding. One hundred percent of the operating budget comes from listener donations. In order to maintain its complete unadulterated freedom in programming, the station does not sell commercials, and it accepts no corporate or government funding. It is run as a democracy, with listeners voting on the budget and attending station meetings.

Harry: *"Like any democracy it can be unwieldy, and conflicts can develop. But overall our vision has been pure, and we have operated in a fiscally responsible manner. We have never been in the red."*

Minot is the only paid staffer. This month he leads a campaign to raise half the yearly budget, with donations pledged by their intensely loyal audience.

Harry: *"We can't be all things to all people, so what we are is something for everybody at different times."*

WPKN—celebrating thirty-five years as something different that is positively Connecticut. ■

ℒISTEN UP:

WPKN 89.5 FM has worldwide listenership via the Internet. If you can't get the station on your radio but have a computer, try www.wpkn.org. Net listeners send in contributions from as far away as Brussels. Prior to the station's Net casts, one Massachusetts fan built a 150-foot tower on his property just so he could pick up its signal.

Other than being a tenant in the University Student Center, the radio station is in no way affiliated with the University of Bridgeport, the Professors World Peace Academy, or the Unification Church, which operate the university. ■

TRAINS: A LOVE STORY

Wallingford

W*hen I heard about Peters' Railroad Museum, I had no idea what to expect. We drove up to a small, unassuming ranch house in Wallingford. But when we got inside, we couldn't believe the magnitude of the collection.*

When we met Dave and Barbara Peters, we knew this was more than a train story. It was a love story.

For Dave Peters the love affair started in elementary school. Sometimes Dave got in trouble with the teacher for watching the trains from his classroom window, but that didn't diminish his love. Instead Dave grew up to be a machinist, working thirty-three years, first for the New Haven Railroad and later for its successor, Amtrak. Dave brought his work home with him, too, collecting so much railroad

memorabilia that he eventually opened a museum in the basement of his home.

Climb down the basement stairs and you'll take a train trip into the past. The entryway is an old-fashioned ticket window that was salvaged when train stations were demolished or modernized. It is outfitted with vintage tickets and the things the stationmaster would have kept on his desk.

Dave: *"The deck is from the Wallingford railroad station, the grill is too. The framing around it is from buildings that were torn down in New Haven."*

Dave shows how conductors passed through the cars offering refreshment, and sometimes something more, to the passengers. He's carrying a vintage canteen and pouring into a rounded cup.

Dave: *"I'd serve you a cup of water. Then you'd drink the water and you'd give it back to me, and I would immediately wipe it out, and somebody else across the aisle would want a drink of water, and I'd give them a glass of water. Meanwhile the first person I gave the water to might have the start of whooping cough or diphtheria or God knows what."*

Another display replicates an elegant dining car. Tables are set with beautiful china and silver, much of it made right here in Connecticut. A six-course meal cost $1.75.

Other remnants of railroading history are stacked on shelves, not far from the washing machine and dryer. There are flags and lanterns used to signal trains and more than forty file drawers of documents, including a deed for steamships signed by railroad baron Cornelius Vanderbilt.

Dave and his wife are railroad archaeologists, spending vacations traveling to the sites of wrecks and derailments, collecting fragments left behind, preserving the history of a form of transportation hardly known today. But the decline of the American railroads isn't the end of the love story. Dave has invented his own railroad and has modeled a town—Oak Creek—for it to run through.

Dave: *"This is a town in Colorado. It's in the coal country."*

In the tiny town of Oak Creek a hot-air balloon is coming in for a landing near the tracks, and circling overhead is a biplane not longer than your finger, with a minuscule aviatrix standing on one wing.

Dave: *"That's John Glenn the astronaut's mother. She was a wing walker right after World War I."*

Dave knows that a fascination with trains is shared by many.

Dave: *"I think most people in America are interested in trains. They make believe they're not, but deep down there's something about a train that gets them."*

Dave Peters loves trains. And he knows the best thing to do with love is to share it. That's what makes Dave Peters's basement museum positively Connecticut. ∎

*𝒰*PDATE:

David and Barbara Peters enjoy hosting individuals and small groups at their museum. Hours are by appointment only. If you'd like to schedule a visit, call (203) 269-1788. David also travels throughout the state to schools and senior centers making presentaions on railroad history. To learn more, visit the museum Web site at pages.cthome. net/petersrrmuseum. ▪

DREAM CATCHER

Madison

People in Connecticut who want to learn more about Native Americans might head to the Mashantucket Pequot Museum and Research Center, right near the Foxwoods Resort Casino. But for many years a Madison woman has been quietly passing on the traditions of Native Americans with her own two hands.

The slender bit of vine woven in a circle looks as if a spider has used it as a frame to spin its web. Fixed in its strands is a bright bit of turquoise. The web is not a spider's trap for catching insects; this delicate device is for catching dreams. The dream catcher was fashioned by Dale Carson, who loves to share the lore and legend of her Native American heritage. Dale explains that dream catchers were often hung over a cradle to protect a child from bad dreams. She decorates them with feathers and bits of turquoise for luck.

Dale: *"The idea is to keep the bad spirits away while you're dreaming so that you only dream good dreams. Then in the morning all the bad dreams that are caught in the web are burned up by the sun."*

Dale is a member of the Abenaki nation and an authority on Woodland cultures. And although Dale is a lecturer and writer, she prefers to express her Native American background through crafts and through cooking.

There are different ways of passing on tradition, Dale says.

Dale: *"Some are natural born writers or storytellers. Me, I'm a cook."*

So Dale dishes up oppenonauhoc (oyster) stew and nepeshwaog (wild fowl) with apricot sauce or pemmican, a jerky made from buffalo, venison, rabbit, or squirrel with fat, nuts, and berries pounded into its surface. Dale has compiled her recipes in two Native American cookbooks, which she says she thinks of as "a bridge, a means of reintroducing Native American food and culinary traditions into mainstream kitchens." She might include exotic ingredients—like buffalo meat in a ragout—or offer complete instructions

for a clambake. Although we often think of clambakes as a New England tradition, they originated with the Pequots and other tribal nations who lived here long before Europeans arrived.

Dale often speaks at local schools and is now working with another Native American friend on a book for children. The book is based on traditional Native American tales, such as "How the Cheyenne Girl Saved Her Brother." Each story will be paired with a recipe kids can cook, like "Horses Love Oats-meal Cookies."

That's how Dale Carson is preserving the old ways in a present that's positively Connecticut. ■

𝒮INCE OUR STORY:

Dale's cookbook New Native American Cooking *is published by Random House. Dale's other books,* Native New England Cooking *and* The Dream Catcher Book *are available through the Institute for American Indian Studies in Washington, Connecticut. Dale makes Native American crafts (shields and "talking sticks") to sell at the institute, the Abbe Museum in Acadia National Park in Maine, Yale's Peabody Museum in New Haven, and the Smithsonian Institution in Washington, D.C. Dale is seen in a film about Native American cuisine that's part of the exhibit at the Mashantucket Pequot Museum and Research Center.* ▢

PUPPET MASTERS

Storrs & Mansfield

Deep in the basement of a dormitory at the University of Connecticut in Storrs, life is beginning. Not in a biology lab, but in a puppet lab, where students are breathing life into a strange cast of characters.

Deborah Hertzberg: *"This is a fruit-faced Chihuahua."*

Amy Weinstein: *"This is a water mystic/water shaman."*

CJ McLaughlin is constructing an Indonesian-style shadow puppet. And Jason Hines is draping a huge puppet form over his slender body.

Jason: *"This is another version of the Dr. Faustus character."*

They are students in UConn's puppetry program, the only one in the country offering three degrees—Bachelor of Fine Arts, Master of Arts, and Master of Fine Arts.

Deborah already has a degree in acting but explains why she has moved to puppetry.

Deborah: *"As an actress I'm limited to this body and this voice. As a puppeteer I can be a mambo Chihuahua or I can be anything! It's far more creative, and there are far more opportunities."*

Although some on campus have never heard of it, the program is renowned among puppeteers, in large part because of its founder, Frank Ballard, and its only professor, Bart Roccoberton.

Bart: *"Most days as I walk down the stairs to this space there is a creative energy that's pounding up the staircase that is so inviting and so reviving. I love working here."*

He's loved working here for twenty-five years, if you count his time as a student and as a teacher. Bart recruits students far and wide. He met Hua Hua Zhang, a leading performer with a top Chinese puppet troupe, when he was producing a TV show in Beijing.

Bart: *"For twenty years she had been a*

performer, only a performer. In that TV project she watched me write, direct, design, build, even load the truck and drive it. She said, 'I want to do that too!'"

Hua Hua knew UConn was the place to learn those skills, but her salary amounted to only $400 a year in American money. So Bart appealed to the university.

Bart: *"I finally said, 'Look, this woman is known throughout the art form in China. She works on Chinese TV. Through this one individual you can have an effect on a quarter of the world's population.'"*

The university agreed. Hua Hua got a scholarship to write, produce, and direct an original puppet play, "The Bell," as her master's thesis. She tells a little about its ideas.

Hua Hua: *"I always wish the world is peaceful and the people love each other. But sometimes, unfortunately, there is a misunderstanding and the people start fighting. Then war happens, and this scares me."*

As his thesis, Jason Hines of North Carolina is producing his own take on the legend of Faustus.

Jason: *"He's a man who sells his soul to the devil and gets all this worldly power and fame. But I thought it got kind of boring in the middle and very philosophical, so I decided to replace all that with a big fight scene at the end. It kind of turns into a Godzilla movie."*

Over the years the UConn students created so many puppets for productions on campus that the puppeteers ran out of places to put them. So UConn opened a puppet museum nearby at the former Mansfield Training School.

Frank Ballard, who founded the puppetry program at UConn in the 1950s, is the curator. Although Parkinson's disease forced his retirement from the university and from performing, Frank oversees the museum, mounting exhibits and mustering the dexterity to restore the matchstick-sized characters a Chaplin man created to perform operas at his home. Frank attended many of those performances by Sidney Chrysler, a dedicated hobbyist.

Frank: *"It was exactly the same as a live opera. After ten minutes you couldn't tell whether you were in Chrysler's studio or in the Metropolitan Opera's second balcony, mainly because he had everything so perfectly designed that it was exact scale."*

When Frank retired in 1989, the puppetry program was nearly eliminated, but political and university leaders were deluged with letters of support

sent from around the world. Puppetry was reinstated, and Bart was hired to run the program.

Bart: *"There are two generations of kids in this nation who have learned how to read because of the alumni of this program working on Sesame Street. Virtually every special effects film from the first Star Wars has involved alumni in one way or another."*

ℳORE DETAILS:

The Ballard Institute and Museum of Puppetry is open April through November on Friday, Saturday, and Sunday from noon to 5:00 P.M. For directions or information about exhibits, group tours, or special events, call (860) 486–4605. For information about the Puppetry Program, visit the UConn School of Fine Arts Web site: www.sfa.uconn.edu. ■

And then there are alumni working on and off Broadway, and using puppets in therapy with troubled kids.

UConn has helped Jason Hines hone his skills.

Jason: *"Pretty much everyone in the puppetry world knows that this is the place to study to get formal training in puppet arts."*

And the place to see his version of Faust's bargain with the devil carried out in a big way, with a cast of fifty and puppets as big as 20 feet tall, all ending in a hellish blaze, a bonfire that consumes all the puppets and props at the end of his show.

The puppetry program at UConn, a place to carry out a creative vision that is positively Connecticut. ■

Yankee Ingenuity

RIDING THE NAUGY'S RAILS

S *ince 1968 the Railroad Museum of New England has been collecting New England train cars (known as rolling stock) and railroad artifacts dating from the 1840s, including everything from tickets to signal towers to the photo archive of the New Haven Railroad. Now the railroad buffs who started the museum are really having fun. They're running a real railroad!*

The Naugy lives again. In 1995, exactly 150 years from the chartering of the original railroad line, a dedicated group of men and women, the members of the Railroad Museum of New England, revived the Naugatuck Railroad Company. Jan Harris was one of them.

Jan: *"I just love it! I can't keep away from here. It's just so much fun and the people I work with are wonderful."*

The Naugy now runs nearly 20 miles from Waterbury to Torrington. Passengers ride in restored 1920s-era coaches. Bob Perol is a conductor.

Bob: *"Hi gang! Welcome to the Naugatuck Railroad. Today we have Naugatuck 529, an ex-New Haven locomotive that used to run in the 1950s and '60s on this very line between Waterbury and the top of the line, which was Winsted. All these coaches have been painstakingly restored to better than their original condition."*

The railroad is really a mobile museum staffed and supported by 400 volunteers.

Jan: *"We do all sorts of work, from being engineers to being conductors and car hosts, to painting equipment to hammering spikes and ties—wherever we're needed."*

The ride from Thomaston to the Waterville section of Waterbury traces some of the prettiest countryside in the valley, winding through the Mattatuck State Forest and the Litchfield Hills and crossing the Naugatuck River three times.

The railroad has over ninety pieces of rolling stock, including several locomotives, and nearly every type of railroad car: freight cars, passenger cars, a snowplow, a working crane, cabooses. The history of the original railroad follows the industrial development in the valley, and its demise. John Gamm is the executive director of the museum.

John: *"There were no subsidies for passengers then. The railroad was running untold numbers of people into Grand Central and into Boston and losing money on every passenger. Then I–95 came along, which took more people out of the passenger cars and more freight out of the freight cars."*

With Connecticut's conversion to a service economy, there's just not as much freight to haul. But these days the Naugatuck carries something even more precious: history—making the Naugatuck Railroad Company positively Connecticut. ■

*M*ORE:

Currently the museum is restoring the Thomaston station, built in 1881. Eventually it hopes to re-create a 1920s atmosphere and give visitors a glimpse into an era when life in New England towns centered around the local train station.

In addition to its regular excursions, the Naugatuck Railroad offers the only wine train in the east. Special trains run from Thomaston to the East Litchfield station, where passengers catch a bus to Haight Vineyard for a tour, tasting, and music. Along the way the train offers light fare, wine, and live entertainment.

The Naugatuck Railroad also offers licensed drivers over the age of eighteen the chance to be an engineer for an hour. For a fee of $250 you can test your skills at the throttle of a real locomotive! ▪

THE CHEESE LADY

*W*isconsinites may call themselves cheese heads, and Vermont is known for cheddar, but at Cato Corner Farm, you'll find gourmet cheeses that are positively Connecticut.

Liz MacAlister loves her cows, the Holsteins, Guernseys, and brown Swiss. Some of them, like Gossamer Bee, are named after characters in the Dylan Thomas play "Under Milk Wood." China Doll got her name from a Grateful Dead tune.

Twice a day Liz and her border collie, Ike, round them up on her Cato Corner Farm in Colchester. Liz milks the herd, and spring through fall she reserves most of the raw milk to make European-style aged cheeses.

Liz: *"I wish I could remember who said 'Cheese makes milk immortal.'"*

Liz has been making cheese for about fifteen years, but she started commercial production only a few years ago. Making such a value-added product at the farm was the best way she could think of to keep her herd.

Liz: *"There's no way with eighteen, twenty, thirty cows that I could make a living, because the price of milk is just not high enough. But if I can make a product that I can sell at a much higher value, a more sophisticated product, then I can make a living, and that's where it's at."*

Cheese making is a six-hour process that starts with cold milk being pumped into a vat, and then warmed to about 80 degrees.

Liz: *"Then I add culture. Culture is a lacto bacterium. There are different ones, and they determine the flavor of the cheese after it's aged."*

When it ripens, Liz adds rennet, an enzyme that causes the milk to coagulate and separate into solids, called curds, and liquid, called whey. The curds are scooped into cheese forms, then

pressed, flipped, and turned. Hours later wheels of cheese are removed, then stored and aged at least four months. The taste develops as the cheese ages.

Liz: *"The lacto bacilli, which are the milk cultures, develop in different ways according to type of cheese, and their interaction with fat in the milk."*

Liz makes cheddar, brown cow Swiss, Belgian abbey, Dutch farmstead, and Montasio varieties. They are handmade cheeses with distinct flavors, different from mass-produced cheeses.

Liz: *"The whole mass-production process is very standardized, whereas when I make a cheese, the seasonal variations in the milk are very important. The cheese made in the spring is very unlike the cheese I make in the fall."*

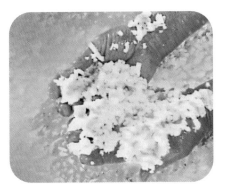

Liz makes cheese only when her cows are turned out to graze.

Liz: *"The cheese produced from milk when the cows are on pasture is better than cheese produced when they are on silage, which is a common winter feed."*

Other ingredients in the recipe . . . tradition and pride.

Liz: *"There's a lot of pleasure in working with cows, being in a natural setting, and producing a product that's your own."*

A handmade farm product that is positively Connecticut. ∎

𝒮INCE OUR STORY:

Liz has added some new varieties to her cheese offerings, including Myfanwye's Caerphilly, a traditional Welsh cheese that's really popular. Her son Mark is now helping market the cheese and is studying to become a cheese maker.

Cato Corner cheese is sold locally at some farmer's markets and at Lyman Orchards in Middlefield. New Yorkers love Cato Corner cheeses: Liz sells over one hundred pounds a day at an open-air market in Union Square. ∎

CAR WAX TO THE STARS' CARS

Killingworth & North Branford

I f you are a real car nut, then nothing's too good for your vehicle. That's how Charles Bennett felt when he developed Zymöl, the world's most expensive car wax. And judging by how his company is growing, Bennett was right on the money.

Would you spend $1,500 on a jar of wax for your car? You might if you owned a 1934 one-of-a-kind baby Rolls Royce.

Prices for Charles Bennett's Zymöl waxes start at $45 but can go into the stratosphere for special formulations.

George Dragone is a vintage car dealer.

George: *"It's something in the wax that's just like nothing else. This just seems to bring out the color. That's all we're using now."*

Dragone used Zymöl to restore the twenty-year-old paint on a rare Cobra sports car, now gleaming with a finish you can see your reflection in. Car magazines have described Bennett's invention as a fruit salad car wax.

Chuck Bennett: *"We use banana oil, we use evergreen oil, we use sunflower, montan, safflower, apricot kernel oil, vanilla bean oil, cinnamon bark oil."*

He even got me to taste some of it! But what could possibly make a jar of car wax worth hundreds or even thousands of dollars?

Chuck: *"Quality, and one of the major ingredients in our products is time. Every batch is tended to as though it were the first batch of wax we were ever going to make and as if it were the last batch of wax we were ever going to make."*

Chuck whipped up the first batches in his kitchen in a coffeepot. Now the waxes are mixed in North Branford, in a converted barn, in batches so small the company uses a kettle meant for making spaghetti sauce and a hand ladle to fill the specially designed containers.

Chuck based Zymöl on a 115-year-old formula used on carriages in a small town in Germany.

Chuck: *"I found this product there that was actually made of different kinds of animal fats, which sort of turned me off in the beginning, because I am a vegetarian."*

So Chuck replaced animal fats with plant oils, including carnauba imported from Brazil. Carnauba comes from a palm tree and is widely used in cosmetics. Chuck thinks of your car's paint as a living, breathing skin. His "car cosmetic," he says, will restore suppleness to the paint so it will expand and contract with the car's body, keeping the paint from drying out and cracking.

Different Zymöl waxes are formulated for different painted finishes, ranging from hot rods to new Japanese imports to vintage model Ts. For serious car fanciers, Chuck blends custom waxes.

Chuck: *"We made a custom formulation for a 1929 Rolls based on its condition today. We considered how brittle the paint was, how dense it was, how much color it had lost, what the continual pigment content of the paint was today."*

He even takes into account the weather on the day your car was painted. Custom formulas have cost as much as $16,000. For fashion designer Ralph Lauren it was worth every penny when his 1938 Bugatti took a coveted international prize.

That victory put Zymöl on the map as an elite car care company that's positively Connecticut. ∎

ℐINCE OUR STORY:

Zymöl has grown 500 percent in the last six years. There are now 120 different products in the line, distributed worldwide with offices in Sydney, Singapore, Tokyo, Zurich, Munich, London, Stockholm, and Puerto Rico. Zymöl has been voted the number one car wax by a leading consumer magazine.

Zymöl makes waxes just for sports utility vehicles, boats, and airplanes and offers something special for collectors of rare and expensive cars. Zymöl Vintage Estate Glaze costs $1,650 and is based on a formula developed for a 1947 Bentley Mark VI Cabriolet. The wax arrives in a gleaming carved Lucite container that Zymöl promises to refill for life, at no charge. Customers include celebrity car collectors like Arnold Schwarzenegger, Jay Leno, Tom Hanks, Francis Ford Coppola, and George Lucas.

For more information, you can reach the company via its Web site at www.zymol.com or through the customer service line at (800) 999-5563. ∎

THE SMALLEST SHOW ON EARTH

I n sixty-three years, Bill Brinley produced two miniature circuses—carving, stitching, and handbuilding every element from the tents to the horses and elephants to the spangled ladies dangling from the flying trapeze.

Bill Brinley carved his first circus wagon at the age of nine.

Bill: *"My father would get up and before he went to work he would drop me off down on Dixwell Avenue in New Haven. I'd have a lunch bag, a notebook, and a Brownie camera. I would take pictures of circus wagons and trains in those days."*

Bill used those notes, sketches, and photos to create his own circuses—miniature versions outfitted with authentic scale models of vintage tents and wagons, and populated by teeny versions of real circus people.

All circuses travel, and Brinley's was no exception. His first circus had been to the Steel Pier in Atlantic City, a Las Vegas casino, and the 1964 World's Fair before finally finding a permanent home at the Barnum Museum in Bridgeport, where it takes up much of the third floor.

In P. T. Barnum's day, the big top seated 10,000 people, and there were other tents for his sideshow and the menagerie. Bill has re-created those, too. He estimates that he has carved more than half a million pieces for his two circuses.

Diane: *"Why didn't you ever run away and join the circus?"*

Bill: *"They never did pay very high, and to be frank, I could make more money with my miniatures than they could pay."*

But he's satisfied with the choice he made.

Bill: *"It's kind of unusual to be able to do work that you really enjoy, and I have all my life."*

It has been a life with the circus that's positively Connecticut. ■

ℳORE:

Brinley's circus is just one of the exhibits at the Barnum Museum in Bridgeport, which is devoted to circus impresario Phineas T. Barnum, a native of Bethel and one-time mayor of Bridgeport. Last year when the A&E Network cast Beau Bridges to star in the miniseries P. T. Barnum, *Bridges immersed himself in the museum's collection and library archives for two days as he prepared for the role. He pored over Barnum's letters and diaries, and listened to the showman's voice on one of the first audio recordings ever made. He even visited the grave at Mountain Grove Cemetery where Barnum is buried opposite one of his greatest stars, Tom Thumb.*

To show his thanks to the museum staff for their help, Bridges arranged for A&E to hold a sneak preview of the miniseries in Bridgeport at the newly renovated Polka Dot Playhouse. Beau and his wife, Wendy, attended the black-tie affair and mingled with the guests. Thanks to his appearance, the museum raised more than $50,000. ■

HE SHELLS

W e may go crazy now for our UConn Huskies on the basketball court, and colleges fill their football stadiums with loyal alumni, but the oldest intercollegiate sport, the one that predates basketball and football, is rowing.

Rowing is an old sport, but today the competition is reaching a futuristic level.

Mike Vespoli: "It's a bit like the arms race. You have one that's better and faster, then everyone wants that, until something else better and faster comes along."

What's come along are Vespoli's racing shells, made in New Haven. The former Olympian has radically altered the shape and performance of racing shells with the infusion of aerospace technology—the same technology that allowed Bert Rutan to fly his lightweight plane Voyager around the world nonstop.

Mike holds up a piece of notepaper to demonstrate.

Mike: "If you took a piece of paper, it really has nothing. But if you roll it, it's got a great deal more rigidity. And when you combine that with sandwich construction, you've made something thicker, but using honeycomb you don't make it heavier."

The stiffness of the shell cuts down on the torque and prevents the hull from expanding and contracting as eight oarsmen stroke. That makes the boat faster. So does the smooth enameled bottom. Carbon fibers strengthen the shell, and the honeycombed hull, deck, and bulkhead keep it lightweight. A Vespoli shell is about one hundred pounds lighter than the wooden shells used in the past.

Mike: "I compare it to the stealth bomber in radar. Our hull minimizes the resistance, which affects the speed of the boat. There's a lot of drag on the shell, which can slow it down."

About two hundred of the long, narrow shells are handcrafted at Mike's shop annually. Fully equipped, they even contain specially designed, built-in safety shoes.

Mike: "If the boat tipped over, and it can happen in the smaller boats more than the larger boats, it's important that people can get out quickly. All they have to do now is grab the string with one hand and yank the Velcro releases and their feet would slip right out."

About 70 percent of the eight-man racing shells for U.S. college teams are made by Vespoli. He also produces boats for the Olympics and the Goodwill Games.

Mike Vespoli has another dream he hopes to see fulfilled some day soon. He wants rowing to return to New Haven Harbor, where crew teams have not held races since the 1920s. He'd like to see people of all ages learn to love the sport as he does.

Rowing is a sport that's been changed forever, by a man and a company that are positively Connecticut. ▪

$\mathscr{S}$INCE OUR STORY:

Rowing is growing in popularity, with several area clubs offering classes and competition. The federal Title IX provisions, which guarantee equal opportunity to women in scholastic athletics, have been a boon for the sport on the college level. Many of the major football powers have started rowing for women. The masters market, involving postcollege athletes of all ages, is growing too.

Vespoli now makes 435 boats a year, still the crème de la crème of racing shells. He has upgraded the material for the hull to a unidirectional carbon fiber similar to that used in fighter jets. The company boasts that the U.S. National team has won the championship in a Vespoli shell for three years straight in the Men's Eight competition. In 2000 Vespoli launched what Mike calls the "megasite for rowing" on the Internet. Called irow.com, it is content-driven but includes an electronic pro shop—a place to buy new and used Vespoli shells. ▪

DISNEYLAND OF DAIRY STORES

S tew Leonard says, "You'd have to own a cow to get fresher milk!" But it's more than the milk that brings 100,000 shoppers a week through the doors of Stew Leonard's, "the world's largest dairy store." It's fresh delicious food—and fun!

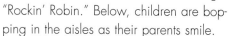

Children pet calves and lambs while chickens squawk and ducks quack in "Stew's Little Farm," positioned just between the store's massive parking lot and Norwalk's busy Post Road. Just outside the store's front door, shoppers line up to lick free ice cream cones, their reward for spending $100 on groceries. And the fun is just beginning!

A robot cow dressed in a Civil War uniform is performing on a stage set atop the frozen food case. The audio-animatronic character sings the fifties rock 'n' roll song

"Rockin' Robin." Below, children are bopping in the aisles as their parents smile.

If it weren't for the shopping carts, you might think you were in Disney World. It's easy to see where dairy store owner Stew Leonard gets inspiration.

Stew: "Walt Disney was one of the greatest men who ever lived. I think in the last one hundred years you could probably count on one hand the people who would be in his category."

The emphasis on fun is one of Stew Leonard's secrets of success. He ticks off the four of them on his fingers.

Stew: "Satisfy the customer. Teamwork. Excellence. The fourth thing is where the fun comes in. W is for 'Make them say WOW.' So the four principles are S-T-E-W, which makes it real easy for me to remember."

The eight-acre Norwalk store is packed with wows, from animated cartons of milk and sticks of butter singing above the dairy case to the petting zoo for the kids. *Ripley's Believe It or Not* pronounced Stew Leonard's "the world's largest dairy store," and at its heart is a milk-processing plant where you can watch your milk being pasteurized. That's how it all began. In 1969 Stew, a milkman then, opened his first dairy store with a window to the milk plant.

These days you can also watch the bakers turn out more than 75,000 croissants a week, as well as a full array of gourmet bakery products. Employees dressed in cow and chicken costumes roam the aisles, sometimes handing out chocolate chip cookies warm from the oven.

All four of Stew's children work here, and the family theme carries over to the rest of the staff. Half of the 600 employees have a relative working in the store.

That makes sense, Stew says.

Stew: *"If a mother is a good worker, and she wants her daughter to come here to work, the odds are that the apple didn't fall far from the tree. Not only will the daughter be a good employee but she will have two bosses—me and her mom."*

Jill Leonard Tavello says employee morale is the key to their success.

Jill: *"My Dad always says, 'A pat on the back is only a few vertebrae above a kick in the pants, but it's a mile apart in the results that it brings.'"*

Stew Leonard's business philosophy is carved in stone, literally, on a giant rock displayed just inside the front door. It says: RULE #1. THE CUSTOMER IS ALWAYS RIGHT. RULE #2. IF THE CUSTOMER IS EVER WRONG, REREAD RULE #1.

That philosophy made a milkman into a millionaire. It is the reason for a prominently displayed suggestion box, and it's why each morning the managers read the customers' suggestions.

One shopper: *"The customer is treated with a kind of respect that is unfortunately a disappearing concept in this country. I think people feel if they have something to say here, the owner is prepared to listen."*

While the average supermarket stocks some 15,000 items, Stew Leonard's only has 1,000, so most shoppers still have to make a stop somewhere else. But the Leonards have bred loyalty in their customers through low prices, excellent quality, and great service. That loyalty shows when shoppers carry their distinctive shopping bags to the four corners of the earth. The snapshots they send back from their travels are pinned to a billboard as a tribute to the "Disneyland of Dairy Stores," a shopping experience that is positively Connecticut. ■

*S*INCE OUR STORY:

Two new stores have opened in Danbury and Yonkers. Stew Leonard Jr. is now in charge of the company. In 1993 Stew Leonard Sr. was found guilty of income tax evasion and served forty-four months in prison. So many other corporations want to know the secrets of the dairy stores' customer service success that Jill Leonard Tavello runs Stew U., a seminar that brings in managers from as far away as Japan. ■

WITCH'S BREW

A weather vane depicting a witch riding a broomstick flaps in the breeze. Despite the witch flying over the E. E. Dickinson Plant in Essex, witch hazel lotion was not first brewed in a witch's cauldron, but by an Indian medicine man.

According to the stories told around here, Indians saw the flowering witch hazel bush and it intrigued them, so they boiled up some of the chips and used the solution to treat wounds. The herbal remedy was soon copied by Connecticut's early settlers, according to Richard Kirpas, who works at E. E. Dickinson.

Richard: *"The white person, when he came over here, he had no real remedies other than leeches and bloodletting. There were no antibiotics or anything."*

In the 1860s, The Reverend Thomas Dickinson capitalized on the witch hazel growing wild in the state.

Richard: *"Mr. Dickinson was a Baptist minister and he was involved with selling shoddy and uniforms to the Union troops during the Civil War. But he was a real businessman— actually he was more of a businessman than a minister."*

Thomas Dickinson's son Edward Everett Dickinson built his father's company into a nationwide supplier of witch hazel lotion. The Dickinson family guided the business for decades, and by the 1930s it had become the nation's biggest producer of the lotion. As their vintage advertisements attest, the product was relied on by women as a beauty aide.

Richard: *"When I first came to work here I looked at samples that go back thirty and forty years that were preserved, and basically the product*

as it is made today is the same as it was in the 1930s and '40s."

Richard oversees distillation in a plant that's right out of the 1920s, but with equipment that's state-of-the art. The process is simple. The bush is harvested in winter. Twigs and small branches are shredded and loaded into stills, where heat and pressure extract the oils and tannins. Those are added to alcohol, a preservative that has replaced rum, which was used at one time.

The Dickinson plant isn't very big, but they sure do make a lot of witch hazel lotion. Twenty-six storage tanks hold over three-quarters of a million gallons of the stuff. From here it is piped underground about a quarter of a mile to the bottling plant.

Consumers buying witch hazel today use it mainly for skin care. Other companies add it to nearly four hundred cosmetics and skin care products. The real appeal of witch hazel is its steady reliability over the years. Your mother used it to cool your childhood sunburns, your grandmother used it to take the sting out of bug bites.

Richard: *"Customers range anywhere from fifteen to one hundred years old, and we have as many senior citizens using the product as there are young girls using the product."*

Its longevity is part of what makes witch hazel lotion positively Connecticut. ■

*U*PDATE:

E. E. Dickinson had a brother, T. N. Dickinson, who produced witch hazel from a different formula in East Hampton, Connecticut. In 1997 the Dickinson brands merged, and both formulas are now produced at the East Hampton plant. The eleven-acre plot of land and the buildings at E. E. Dickinson's Essex site were sold. Jennifer McCann of Macbeth Ventures is redeveloping the property as The Witch Hazel Works, which will include office space, shops, entertainment, and gallery space, preserving the old buildings for a new era. ■

PEZ

Pez is one of Connecticut's most popular homegrown products, but since it is produced in an FDA-regulated plant, the company is not open to the public for tours. So if you are a Pez lover, here's your chance for a peek inside a novelty that's positively Connecticut.

When Stephen King wanted to evoke childhood memories in his semiautobiographical film *Stand by Me*, he had the youngsters swear their devotion to cherry Pez. Stephen King isn't the

only baby boomer who feels nostalgic about Pez. The candy has been a hit since it was introduced into the United States in 1952. Pez sales keep climbing, and this year more than three billion Pez candies will be consumed in this country alone. And that's without any advertising!

Pez is sold in more than sixty countries, but the fruit-flavored tablet-shaped candies are made in Orange, in a plant that doubled in size twice during the 1990s. Cherry-flavored Pez has been replaced by strawberry; Pez also makes grape, orange, and lemon.

Of course what makes Pez, Pez is the dispenser—and there wasn't one at the beginning, according to Scott McWhinnie, the executive who calls himself the "Pez-ident."

Scott: *"The first candy was developed in 1927 in Vienna, Austria, and it was first marketed as a compressed peppermint candy. Pez came from the German name for peppermint, which is* pfefferminz*. In 1950 the first Pez dispenser was developed, but the early ones were made without character heads."*

But since the fifties, kids have collected the character head dispensers. And there have been hundreds of them.

Scott: *"The most popular characters have been the Disney characters as well as the seasonal characters, like Santa Claus and Easter Bunny."*

At any one time there are dozens of different dispensers in the stores. Pez only occasionally brings back a popular model from the past, so most earlier ones are

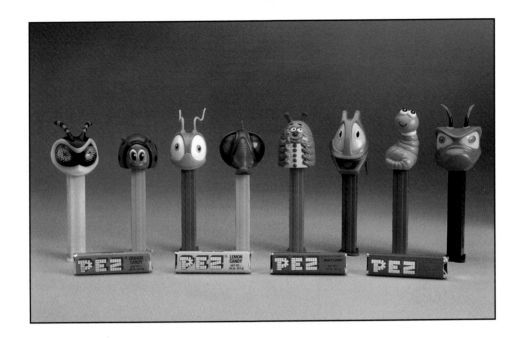

rare and increase in value. Collecting them has become serious business. In five major conventions across the nation each year, collectors buy and sell rare dispensers and other Pez paraphernalia. An original 1960s Psychedelic Eye might be worth a few thousand dollars.

The dispensers change frequently to reflect popular TV shows, movies, or trends. Recently the Simpsons became the latest in candy collectibles from Pez, a product that's positively Connecticut. ■

𝒮INCE OUR STORY:

Pez recently granted use of its name and image to over forty licensees who produce (among other things) T-shirts, watches, eyeglasses, snow globes, tapestries, and Popsicles. Pez dispensers have become so popular there is even a museum devoted to them in Burlingame, California, near San Francisco. The official company Web site offers Pez and Pez-related products at www.pez.com, but there are about sixty unofficial sites maintained by Pez-maniacs. ■

THE HERBAL TOUCH

More and more people are relying on herbs as part of their daily health regimen or as inspiration in cooking. No matter what your reason, you'll find Connecticut herbalists to cater to your needs.

When Valerie Hawk Hoffman was diagnosed with high blood pressure at the age of twenty-two, her doctor recommended beta blockers.

Valerie: *"I thought, I cannot keep putting this synthetic chemical into my body and expect my liver and the rest of my system to treat me respectably."*

Instead Valerie changed her life. She went to an herbalist and, combining herbs with meditation, dramatically lowered her blood pressure.

Valerie: *"I told myself there's something to this, and I quit my job and went to school for herbalism, because I really was determined to spread the word as to how a healthy plant can heal the body."*

Valerie now advises others from her Sunrise Herb Farm in Bethel. She sells dozens of herbal products, extracts, and teas from a shop built by her husband as a replica of Mount Vernon. Trained herbalists make extracts fresh daily. Sunrise specializes in medicinal remedies for everything from the flu to depression. Some medical doctors have asked Valerie to assist in caring for their patients.

Valerie believes herbs can enhance all parts of your life, and she offers classes on a range of topics that include seasonal wellness, aging, weight loss, healing, cooking, and gardening. Her husband, Dave, is a profession-

ally trained chef, specializing in vegetarian cooking. Together they've created recipes for everything from lavender cookies to herbal skin toners and bath salts.

Visit their farm in season, and you can stroll the gardens, enjoying views of the fountain and the resident sheep. The Sunrise Herb Farm, a place for health that is positively Connecticut. ■

ORE:

Sunrise Herb Farm is located at 35 Codfish Hill Road in Bethel. For information call (203) 794–0809. ■

HERBARY HAVEN
Pomfret

At the opposite end of the state, in the far northeast corner, is Martha's Herbary, where Martha Paul has combined her love for cooking with her love of gardening and herbs.

Martha teaches almost 120 well-attended classes a year in topics ranging from the Art of Baking Bread to Spirited Soups and Mother's Day Wreath Making. At various times she's putting up herb-spiced vinegars, cordial, and wines. For the truly herb-inspired, Martha offers an eight-month herbal apprentice-

ship. Give her one Sunday a month, and Martha will take you on a journey into the fascinating world of herbal gardening, decorating, medicine, and cuisine.

Martha has teamed up with two local B&Bs to offer gourmet getaway weekends. During the hands-on classes students prepare a gourmet Provence, Tuscan, or Thai dinner, then enjoy their feast in the dining room of Martha's antique home, which dates to 1780. Her shop is packed with herbal gifts, books, dried arrangements, and gardening items. In the raised beds in her garden Martha grows culinary herbs. Two koi ponds frame the sunken medicinal garden. A formal flower garden and a lavender hedgerow complete the setting.

Martha's Herbary is at 589 Pomfret Street in Pomfret. For information call (860) 928–0009. ■

BUILDING BLOCKS

Branford

T he Stony Creek section of Branford is quiet today, but for nearly 150 years the waterfront village bustled with quarry workers. At the beginning of the twentieth century, more than half its residents (called "Creekers") had jobs directly related to the stone business. Although most of the quarries are quiet now, Creekers are celebrating their heritage. The Stony Creek Granite Quarry Workers Celebration was the first community event in Connecticut recognized by the White House as an official Millennium Project.

From the base of the Statue of Liberty to Grand Central Station, from a bank building and federal office complex in New Haven to the Civil War monument at West Point, the pink granite of coastal Connecticut is seen across the United States.

In the early 1900s twenty quarries in Stony Creek and Guilford employed thousands of workers. Many of them came from Italy, Ireland, Sweden, Finland, England, Scotland, and Spain.

Stephen Castellucci operates the last working quarry, Castellucci Stone International. He is a fifth-generation stonecutter, and his company dates back to 1887.

Stephen: "My grandfather was in the granite business, back in Italy, and so were his father and his father before him. When they came to this country, the stone business was in Maine. From Ellis Island in New York they emigrated to Maine, and from Maine to the Connecticut coastline."

Granite has been quarried here for more than a century, and the evidence is everywhere in the pretty village.

Stephen: "Back in the 1800s there were a lot of little tiny quarries in Stony Creek that were family owned. They didn't have concrete so they used the stone to make the foundations of half the houses in Stony Creek. They quarried the cellar, then used that stone to build the foundation for the house."

John Barnes is known as "The General." He is an ex-Marine who started swinging

a jackhammer here twenty-nine years ago. Now he's the superintendent at Castellucci Stone. The General says the quarrier's life is dirty, noisy, and backbreaking.

Diane: *"What do you look for in a quarryman?"*

John: *"Lots of muscle, and some brains."*

But the work today, aided by diamond-tipped saws and other advanced equipment, is less brutal and more efficient than it was decades ago. In a busy season a dozen workers at Castellucci can harvest more granite than could all the quarries in Stony Creek combined in 1900.

During the 1970s, as glass architecture became popular for skyscrapers and other large buildings, the local stone industry experienced a lull. Ironically the architect who led the trend back to granite is the same one who first experimented with glass. When Philip Johnson chose Stony Creek pink for the façade of the AT&T headquarters in Manhattan, he revived interest in the stone.

Recently orders for Stony Creek granite have shot up again, partly due to a building boom, and partly thanks

ℳORE ABOUT STONE:

The Stony Creek Granite Quarry Workers Celebration includes discussions, lectures, field trips, oral history, a coffee-table book, and a memorial of old granite pieces to be erected outside Willoughby Wallace Memorial Library. For more information write to Stony Creek Granite Quarry Workers Celebration, P.O. Box 3047, Stony Creek, CT 06405. ■

to the stone's beauty—its rich pink color flecked with black and gray.

Stephen: *"It has what we call a variegated grain or sweep, a sweeping effect, of veins in the stone itself, giving each panel life to it."*

To keep up with demand, Castellucci is installing a new system, moving from derricks and cranes to front-end loaders that quickly take out the massive twenty-one-ton blocks. Still, Stephen thinks the site has many more years of life left.

Stephen: *"My children's children will not see the end of the stone that we are standing on now."*

Stony Creek granite, a building block of distinction around the world that is positively Connecticut. ■

ACROSS THE RIVER

Portland

The Connecticut River town of Portland is also promoting its quarry heritage. The brownstones of New York and Boston were built with stone quarried in Portland. The quarries, located near the Arrigoni Bridge, once employed 1,500 workers and helped promote shipbuilding as a major area industry: Ships were needed to transport the blocks of stone all over the country and even to Europe. Portland brownstone is seen in local churches and statues, and in some buildings on the campus of Wesleyan University across the river in Middletown.

The brownstone market declined in the early twentieth century as other less expensive building materials were developed. In 1936 the river flooded the quarries, putting an end to the industry, but recently one small quarry reopened, with a goal of shipping more than 1,250 tons of stone in its first year. The town recently purchased some of the sites along the river, and in May 2000 the Department of the Interior designated two quarries as national landmarks, which may make them a tourist destination in the future.

The Place, Guilford

GRAPE EXPECTATIONS

*I*t took one family ten years to find the right place to make their dream come true. Visitors to Connecticut's Quiet Corner are discovering that dream at one of the state's newest wineries.

On a hillside in Pomfret that has been farmed since 1760 stands a barn that looks as though it might have been there nearly as long. Inside you'll find not hay nor farm animals, but barrels of fine wines, the result of a dream and a family's hobby. Catherine and Steven Vollweiler call their winery Sharpe Hill.

Catherine: *"Twenty years ago when we were younger, I would cook and we would serve the wine that Steven would make in the basement, and people would say, 'You should have a vineyard,' and 'Catherine, you should be a chef.' Eventually we had a dream and an expectation. We followed it and here we are."*

The Vollweilers spent nearly ten years searching New York's Hudson Valley, Long Island, and Connecticut for the right place to combine their passions for antiques, food, and wine. With the help of University of Connecticut scientists, they found the right microclimate at Sharpe Hill.

Catherine: *"You had to have hills for drainage, and it was great to have a mistral, which is a continuous flow of air. You had to have no frost pocketing, and of course you couldn't drop below a certain degree."*

Sharpe Hill's temperature is nearly twenty degrees warmer than average for the area, nurturing Chardonnay, Vignole, Cabernet, and St. Croix varietals.

In the tasting room Catherine's daughter Jennifer offers a wine called Ballet of Angels.

Jennifer: *"This has a taste of grapefruits and oranges, which is all natural—from the grape, no sugar added. It's excellent as an aperitif, or with spicy food. It's one of Connecticut's best-selling wines."*

Its label was derived from a nineteenth-century painting that Catherine had long admired. But it wasn't until she sought permission to use the painting on her label that

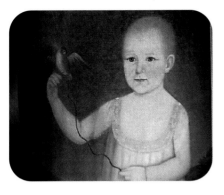

a remarkable coincidence was discovered. Although the painting was owned by a museum in upstate New York, hundreds of miles away, Catherine learned to her amazement that the portrait was of a child who had grown up in Connecticut, right near Sharpe Hill.

Sharpe Hill's red wines and Chardonnay are collecting awards—and fans, like Andy Esposito, who was visiting for the first time from East Haven.

Andy: *"I think the red wines are every bit as good as most of the wines in the Napa Valley of California, and they have the added advantage of having a nice soft finish, so they're wonderful with a meal."*

They're especially wonderful with meals from Catherine's kitchen, based on old family recipes and a lifetime of world travel. In warm weather meals are served outside in a wine garden modeled after some of Catherine's favorite alfresco dining spots in Europe. Inside the replica nineteenth-century cow barn is an inviting early American–style dining room.

*M*ORE:

The wines made at Sharpe Hill are Sharpe Hill Vineyard Chardonnay (gold medal winner, Tasters Guild International), Ballet of Angels, Cabernet Franc, Red Seraph, St. Croix, and Select Late Harvest. In winning the gold medal from the Tasters Guild International, the Vollweilers say their Connecticut Chardonnay beat some of the most popular California wines, including those made by Mondavi, Cakebread, and Sterling Vineyards. The winery expects to release a French-oaked Reserve Chardonnay sometime in 2000. Sharpe Hill is open year-round for tours, tastings, and gourmet dining every Friday, Saturday, and Sunday from 11:00 A.M. to 5:00 P.M. There are two seatings for lunch; reservations are recommended. Private parties and weddings can be arranged in the wine garden or the fireside tavern. For details call (860) 974-3549.

To learn more about Connecticut wines or visiting the state's wineries, check out www.ctwine.com. ■

The attention to detail in the construction and decoration of Sharpe Hill transports guests to an earlier time and place, but the wine making is state of the art. Karen Carpenter leads tours of the winery.

Karen: *"There's such a science to it, even in choosing which oak barrels. There's lightly toasted, medium toasted, American oak, French oak."*

Each adds a different character to the wine. Sharpe Hill is experimenting with a hardy new varietal called the St. Croix. Catherine thinks it could be an alternative crop for struggling farmers in the state.

Catherine: *"They could now grow grapes. Just like the great industry in California, Connecticut could potentially become a magnificent vinicultural state."*

With a reverence for the past, and a vision for the future, the owners of Sharpe Hill Winery are pioneers who are positively Connecticut. ■

$\mathscr{L}$OOKING AHEAD:

Steven Vollweiler is working with the Connecticut Vineyard and Winery Association and the Farm Winery Council to establish more vineyards across Connecticut. The organizations are hoping the state will help with a special loan program. ■

SUITED TO A TEA

Salisbury is a picturesque town in the extreme northwest corner of Connecticut, just 6 miles from the Massachusetts border and within 3 miles of New York State. Many people visit for the scenery; others are drawn by the antiques shops. Then there are those searching for a place that suits them to a "T."

People have been drinking tea for about 5,000 years, and master tea blender John Harney believes tea is enjoying a ren-

aissance in this country. He compares it with Americans' learning about wine in the 1970s.

John: *"The only people who drank wine were either Italians or French or people who traveled a lot. But now you look in a restaurant, and you will see wine on almost every table."*

Then came the craze for bottled water, then upscale coffees. Now, John says, it's tea.

John: *"It's the largest beverage other than water that's drunk around the world. Not in America, though, because if you remember we had a revolution about that. It kind of ruined it for the rest of us here."*

John Harney was introduced to the fine points of tea while managing Salisbury's White Hart Inn. When the inn was sold in 1983, he opened his own tea business, sending his sons Mike and Paul around the world to buy tea leaves from China, India, Taiwan, Japan, Vietnam, and Sri Lanka. The names of the teas resonate like poetry: Assam, Ceylon, Lapsang Souchong, Darjeeling, Oolong.

In a renovated barn, 115 varieties of tea are blended and packed, including loose teas in tins and tea bags individually wrapped and sealed in packets of foil.

Greg Rawlings is blending Earl Grey Supreme, a combination of two Chinese teas—an Assam from India and a tea from Sri Lanka. He stirs in bergamot oil—fragrant and, at $600 per gallon, expensive. This is what separates Harney and Sons

Tea Company from other tea blenders: using the finest teas and the highest quality ingredients, from oils to delicate rosebuds.

Harney and Sons is a boutique operation, selling to upscale hotels like the Four Seasons and gourmet stores like Williams-Sonoma. The company also sells to individual tea lovers through its catalog and Web site. John says one sip is all it takes to sell his tea.

John: *"People are used to having poor quality tea and small amounts of it. You give them the right size bag—thirty-five grains versus twenty-four or twenty-eight grains—and you have 25 to 30 percent more tea. And all of a sudden you raise the quality and people say, 'God, this is great!'"*

If you would like to try a sip, the Harney and Sons tea-tasting room is the place to go. Anyone who has attended a tasting at a winery will understand the concept of a tea tasting. At a wine tasting you work your way from white to red. Tea tasting is similar.

Mike Harney: *"We start with the white teas and then work our way up to the most flavored teas."*

Mike directs tasters to sniff the dry leaves first, then sniff the leaves that have been steeped in hot water.

Mike: *"They say the sign of a good tea taster is a little bit of the tea on the nose. It means you've been very close."*

First we try a slightly sweet silver-tipped Ceylon. The next tea, Japanese genmaicha, is mingled with what appear to be delicate kernels of popcorn.

Mike: *"This is actually popped rice. While the tea is dry, they put in the rice. It dries out the rice and eventually some of the rice pops, so the tea has a definite rice flavor."*

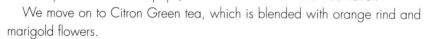

We move on to Citron Green tea, which is blended with orange rind and marigold flowers.

Mike: *"Green tea is very popular because it helps prevent cancer and cardiovascular problems."*

Next, a golden-tipped black tea that looks a bit like pipe tobacco . . . a mangalam Assam from India . . . then a flavored black tea, Cranberry Autumn. Tea tasting takes a little practice—you need to overcome the manners you were taught!

Mike: *"What we try to do is like wine, we aerate the tea (slurp), like that (slurp)."*

I try a tea probably unfamiliar to most of us—Dragon Pearl Jasmine. It has a perfumelike aroma.

Mike: *"When the jasmine flowers bloom in the summertime, the leaves or the flowers are put in with the tea. All of the essence is soaked up by that dry tea."*

We finish with a French herbal tea called Vervaine and then a Mango Fruit tea from Austria.

MORE:

You can reach Harney and Sons at (800) TEA–TIME. ■

In the tasting room Brigitte Harney, Mike's wife, sells teas prepacked or loose, by the ounce or pound.

Brigitte: *"A lot of people buy by the pound, and they come back every three weeks."*

Brigitte stocks the shop with beautiful teapots, cups, tea cozies and measures, even books and stationery. In the back, the staff fills mail orders and makes up lovely gifts packed in hatboxes stuffed with gold tissue and tied with French ribbon. If you're lucky, John Harney might read your tea leaves, as he did mine.

John: *"That's a duck. That means you are coming into wealth."*

I don't know about that, but the tea leaves spell out one message even I can read—Harney and Sons Tea Company is positively Connecticut. ■

ANOTHER TEATIME FAVORITE

Higganum

At Sundial Gardens in the Higganum section of Haddam, the tearoom and tea gift shop are set amid formal gardens, including a Persian-style knot garden, an eighteenth-century-style garden with geometric walkways, and a topiary garden. Ragna Goddard is a tea expert and offers seminars on tea, often followed by exquisite pastries created by her husband, Tom, who is writing a teatime cookbook. Their fine and rare teas are for sale in the shop, along with tea accoutrements and their own scone mixes. You can shop their Web site at www.sundialgardens.com. Sundial can arrange private teas for groups in their garden setting. Phone (860) 345-4290 for hours and days of operation. ■

NEVER ON FRIDAYS

Nothing changes at Blackie's hot dog stand, and that's just the way the customers like it.

Jim Hamilton (Watertown): *"This place is still closed on Friday. And why is it closed on Friday? Because the Catholics in this area couldn't eat meat on Fridays, and it's just tradition."*

Nell Flavin has been serving nothing but hot dogs since 1928, unless you count the occasional hamburger, and

Blackie's has sold those only for the last ten years.

In her Irish brogue, Nell has an explanation for adding hamburgers to the menu.

Nell: *"Because people used to come in and say, 'Oh, I can't eat a hot dog. It comes back on me.' I began to think, now they're good enough to come here, and their other friends are eating*

hot dogs and they can't have anything, so we added the hamburgers."

There are no fries, and no chili, but everybody who eats here tells you to have the relish. There are tubs of it on the countertop so you can help yourself. Nell brought the recipe with her when she came here as a teenager from Ireland. Over there they made it with mushrooms, here they make it with peppers. Nell makes the relish, some 2,500 gallons of it, once a year while sitting under a big tree on a hot summer day. It's been Blackie's trademark since Nell's sister Mrs. Blackman opened the place as a filling station.

Nell: *"She started with one gas tank, and some friend of hers built her a little shack so she could be in out of the cold, and then someone else gave her a potbelly stove, and at night when the customers for the gas came*

by, she would cook and she would say, 'Oh, come on now, you have to have a hot dog or a cup of coffee anyhow.' That's how the business started."

Nell's customers seem like family.

Al Edele: *"It's been many years. I would hate to guess how many; I would venture to say maybe forty or forty-five. I started coming here with my mother and dad."*

Aldo Copes: *"I always order two hot dogs and then I always seem to get just one more. If I can walk out of here with just eating two, then I'm doing pretty good."*

Blackie's, the classic hot dog stand, is a Cheshire landmark that's positively Connecticut. ■

$\mathscr{S}$INCE OUR STORY:

Nell Flavin passed away at the age of eighty-five and now her daughter-in-law Susan runs the hot dog stand. But Susan understands tradition, too, so she's not making any changes. Susan says, "We're planning on doing exactly what we've been doing for seventy-two years!" She still closes on Fridays. She still serves the homemade relish, and she still does not serve fries—no matter how many customers request them! Susan is proud of her family tradition—Blackie's was voted Connecticut's Best Dog by Connecticut *magazine in 1998 and 1999.* ■

TASTE OF THE PAST

Farmington Valley

When snowflakes fall in January, February, and March, several historic sites in the Farmington Valley invite people to gather around the glowing hearth and enjoy a taste of the past. They are part of a wintertime program offered by the Farmington Valley Visitors Association known as Romancing the Past.

A Sunday afternoon tour of Farmington's Stanley Whitman House on High Street includes a look at the gourmet kitchen of the eighteenth century. But when Deacon John Stanley built this New England saltbox, the kitchen wasn't just for cooking. A tour guide explains its function.

Diane Nattrass: *"This is a room from the 1720s. The fireplace hearth was the center of family life. In wintertime the whole family would have slept here. There was no sense of privacy as we have today. Everyone would have brought their straw pallets down from the upstairs chambers, and for warmth they would sleep in front of the fire; that would never go out."*

Deacon Stanley sold the house to Ebenezer Steel, who passed it on to his daughter Mary when she was a newlywed. Mary and Thomas Smith raised five children

there before selling it to Solomon and Susannah Whitman. Both families are remembered in the historic interpretation of the house today. A few pewter mugs and serving pieces, some wooden bowls, and a rolling pin—items from Mary's wedding dowry—line the shelves. Mary Smith and Susannah Whitman fed their families in this kitchen without any of the conveniences we take for granted today.

That's why Judy Witzke enjoys cooking Colonial style over the open hearth. It's a challenge. In the classroom barn building next door, Judy, dressed in Colonial garb, demonstrates the way Smith and Whitman would have prepared a family meal in the eighteenth century. She explains that even though she's using hot coals and cast-iron cookware, as they did, there are similarities to today's cooking methods.

Judy: *"I am preheating my Dutch oven just like you preheat your oven at home."*

Judy took the job teaching 300-year-old cooking arts after being downsized out of a very modern-day job as a computer programmer.

Judy: *"The utensil I am using is called a 'spider.' It's a fry pan with three legs, and it works just like your fry pan at home, but instead of putting it on a burner on top of a stove, I put it on a bed of coals."*

Judy has mastered the switch from high tech to low tech with ease, grace, and a great deal of success, judging by the comments on her apple-sauce fritters, cornbread, and corn chowder.

Ray Guenter of West Hartford was amazed at her ability to create the fritters in the old fireplace.

Ray: *"The idea of being able to produce something like this from something like that boggles the mind."*

Other guests slather their warm cornbread with the sweet butter Judy churned before our eyes, and sip the buttermilk she squeezed from the solids left in the bottom of the churn. Each dish turns out perfectly, but Judy says trial and error has been a big part of adapting these Colonial recipes to modern sensibilities.

Judy: *"We have quite a few recipes in the archives, and some are adapted and modernized versions of Colonial recipes. Their measuring cup wasn't standard like the Pyrex cup that we use. It would have been an ordinary household cup, and it might not have been a true eight ounces."*

Now, Judy says, she finds Colonial-style cooking almost as easy as cooking with her microwave at home, if a bit more time-consuming.

Judy: *"If I were to continue cooking, I would dump coals from on top of my Dutch oven back into the fire and reheat them. The Colonial women would keep using the coals until they burned down to ash, and even then they would not have thrown away the ash. They would have turned that into lye and used it in soap making."*

Early American hearth tours, combining food and fun with history in a way that's positively Connecticut. ∎

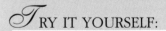

RY IT YOURSELF:

The hearth tours range from a Colonial candlelight dinner to a Victorian tea. For more information contact the Farmington Valley Visitors Association at (800) 4-WELCOME. ∎

LAWN FOOD

O ne of the most unusual lunches I've ever eaten was shared with a dentist who took me grazing, literally, in his backyard, the woods, and a nearby swamp.

When most of us step outside on a nice spring day we see the blossoms, the tinges of green, the new leaves, the beauty of spring. When dentist Warren Koehler goes outside, he may see the same things, but he thinks "dinner." As he strolls around, he's not merely taking a walk. He's foraging.

Warren: *"It sort of means scrounging around, seeing what you can gather for supper. If you were camping, I suppose it might mean collecting frogs or crawfish or something that you could boil up and have for dinner."*

Alongside Warren's house we find some chickweed for salad, and the fiddleheads will be up soon. In the meadow are daylilies.

Warren: *"They are very abundant in Connecticut in the spring. You can see at the roots they are like a little bunch of carrots."*

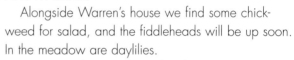

In the woods we find a patch of ramp, something like a wild leek.

Warren: *"It's more of a southern plant than it is here in New England, but this is about the northern-most boundary for it."*

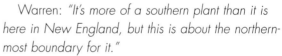

Warren grinds the berries from his spice bush to use in place of pepper, picks catnip leaves for tea, and cuts wintercress for the salad bowl. He has some advice about the wintercress.

Warren: *"Before it blossoms it comes out fine; after it blossoms it comes out bitter."*

Warren finds a lot of his food this way. And his freezer is full of fowl and game, including squirrel and snapping turtle, packed away and labeled in milk cartons.

Warren stalks the wild marsh marigold in the tradition of Euell Gibbons. He harvests cattails, which he says can be boiled like corn on the cob. And there's the wild version of asparagus, Japanese knotweed.

Warren: *"This is delicious when cooked like asparagus. It has a little bit of an acid flavor, and some*

people, in addition to putting butter on it, like to put a little sugar with it."

He warns that you shouldn't try foraging for food on your own because many wild plants can be poisonous. He recommends checking with a local nature center for courses on foraging, like the ones he occasionally teaches.

Warren: *"Actually this is an old Yankee tradition that I'm bringing back. This is why I think you may be right when you say it's positively old-time Connecticut."* ■

ℐIDELIGHT:

Warren Koehler and his wife, Peg, make wine from dandelions and locust pods, and jams from violet blossoms and elderberries. But he admits that she prefers what she calls "civilized food." One night as he dined on squirrel, she had pork chops. ■

WALK ON THE WILD SIDE

Sharon

Dr. Koehler advised checking with a local nature center before eating anything you forage. One place to learn more is the Sharon Audubon Center, a nature and wildlife sanctuary owned by the National Audubon Society. The Center has over 11 miles of scenic hiking trails and more than 750 acres of forest, meadows, wetlands, ponds, and streams. Naturalists and botanists offer educational programs for all ages, and the center has a natural history library. The center holds an annual festival that gathers experts for talks on topics ranging from nature photography to "Everything You Always Wanted to Know about Wildflowers, Ferns, and Mushrooms—But Were Afraid to Ask." For more information call (860) 364-0520. ■

THE ULTIMATE INDULGENCE

Hartford

*I**f you're one of those people who thinks "Life is short—eat dessert first," then you're David Glass's kind of person. Life is too short to miss his yummy treats.***

They're called "the ultimate indulgence," these desserts made by David Glass. His cakes are served in fine restaurants and sold in gourmet stores, but David and his wife, Viv, create them in the old Colt Firearms building in Hartford. They started the business sixteen years ago at home.

David: *"One room had chocolate and boxes. Another room had cakes that were finished."*

But as the mouth-watering word spread, their little company expanded. Desserts By David Glass now employs about thirty people and turns out 100,000 cakes a year. But his signature product is still the same . . . the chocolate truffle cake.

David: *"It's the essence of chocolate. There's no better chocolate product in the world that I've ever tasted."*

David Glass now makes about twenty different cakes, including a cheesecake topped with rich chocolate ganache or flavored with pumpkin or key limes. And there's the Albert Einstein Carrot Cake.

Diane: *"Why do you call it that?"*

David: *"It was the best idea we'd ever come up with—these fresh carrots, these plump raisins, everything just came together so well, that it was like a stroke of genius."*

David calls his Italian almond cake "sublime and seductive," just like its namesake, Sophia Loren.

David: *"When we first started making it, we got a letter from her lawyer saying cease and desist. And we protested to him that we just did this to honor her, we love her so much. And nonetheless, he said, cease and desist. So we came up with an agreement. We pay her a royalty."*

Then there's the product that David invented by accident, literally. He calls them chocolate mousse balls—originally they were molded from pieces of broken chocolate truffle cakes. One new line of cakes is inspired by the Glass children. David dubbed these the Fun Flavor Cakes. One tastes like a Hershey's chocolate bar whipped into a mousse.

Each year David awards a hundred free cakes to the person named the kindest person in the world. When Nelson Mandela won the award, David delivered the cakes, in person, to a fund-raiser in South Africa. Turned out it was a dressy affair, and let's just say David is more of a jeans-and-sneakers kind of person.

David: *"I had to rent a suit, buy some shoes, buy some socks, because I don't own any of that stuff!"*

David donates 25 cents from every Fun Flavor Cake to Mandela's charity for children, and he donates 2.5 percent of his profits to Save the Children, a Westport-based charity. Apparently doing good is also good business. David Glass cakes are now sold with a stock offering attached.

Brad McEwan is the company president: "It's had a tremendous response. Eighty percent of our stockholders are customers who buy our retail cake."

So if you love the cake, you can own part of the company. Desserts By David Glass— they are positively Connecticut. ∎

SINCE OUR STORY:

The deal with Sophia Loren to use her name crumbled, and David announced a contest to rename the cake. First prize: a one-day visit to Hartford, with a promise of all the cakes you can eat, a dinner cooked by David, and a sleepover at the Glass family home. Thousands of entries were sent in. Among David's favorite suggestions: Isabella Rossellini, Madonna, Frank Sinatra, and Joey Buttafuoco. But the winner is The Ultimate Cecilia Bartoli Luscious Chocolate-Covered Italian Almond Cake. The cake is named for the Italian mezzo-soprano, who says she will donate all her royalties to charity. A Canadian woman was the grand prizewinner. ∎

THE PLACE

A rustic eatery in Guilford is a shoreline summertime institution. Summer 2000 marked the thirtieth season in business for the brothers who like to keep The Place pretty much the way it's always been.

As flames lick freshly harvested clams on half shell, I think aloud that this must be the way the first Americans cooked their shellfish, clams, and lobster—roasted over an open fire and served with corn on the cob, grilled right in the husk. Co-owner Gary Knowles agrees.

Gary: "It predates any ovens that I have ever seen."

Cook Kurt Ferguson is lifting lobster on heavy metal racks off the flames.

Kurt: "We use hardwood. It burns with a hot flame and gives a nice charcoal-y taste to the food."

We're at The Place, an outdoor shoreline eatery popular with locals, summer folks, Yalies, and the tourists lucky enough to hear about it. The Place has been around since 1948. In the early days it was located in Madison and was called Whitey's, after the old salt who started it. In 1971 Gary and Vaughn Knowles, schoolteachers and brothers, bought the business, and they have worked hard to retain its original style and atmosphere.

That means open-air and tree-stump seating, with lobster as king. Most diners start with steamers or the roast clams special, served right on the metal grill and eaten with wooden cocktail forks.

The order of the day is BYOB—that's bring your own bottle, your own bread if you want it, and also your own salad and your own side dishes.

Seated comfortably on a big old tree stump, one diner smiles and motions toward the linen place mats his wife has set on the table.

Smiling customer: *"That's what makes it, her place mats. It's just like the Waldorf Astoria, first class!"*

Another customer: *"It's really great. You can just come here on the spur of the moment. Bring your stuff, and have a good time."*

Gary: *"The bottom line is the food is excellent. You can have all the charm in the world, but if you don't have good food, then nobody will come."*

Over the years the brothers have added to the menu. Although half the customers come for lobster, others

enjoy the bluefish, catfish, salmon, steak, and chicken. And more than a few end their meals with mud pie or a hot chocolate sundae.

If The Place feels a little like a big family picnic, well, in a way it is. Many of the customers have been eating here as long as The Place has been around. As high school students, Vaughn Knowles and his wife both worked for Whitey, the founder of The Place.

Vaughn: *"The name came from a poem that Whitey had which was, 'There's no place just like this place anywhere near this place, so this must be the place.'"*

It must be the place that's positively Connecticut. ■

SMOKED

O*n Route 63 just north of the rotary in Goshen, among the hills and farm fields of Litchfield County, is an old-fashioned New England smokehouse run by the Nodine family. Their tasty treats make a fine picnic or an elegant holiday dinner.*

Ronnie Nodine is talking about pigs. Growing them, getting them, smoking them.

Ronnie: *"You'd be surprised where people grow them—in their garage, in their*

cellar. I pick them up from all over the place. I like to say, though, that if you are going to grow a pig, it's either a cheap hobby or expensive meat."

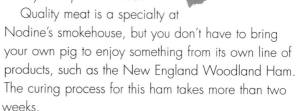

Quality meat is a specialty at Nodine's smokehouse, but you don't have to bring your own pig to enjoy something from its own line of products, such as the New England Woodland Ham. The curing process for this ham takes more than two weeks.

Ronnie: *"We pump them with brine, in and around the bone. Then we take them off the table, rub them with dry cure, put them in a barrel, and let them set for a few days."*

Then the ham is rubbed again and set in a barrel for at least five more days before being washed and smoked for twenty-four hours. The aging makes the difference in flavor.

Ronnie: *"Canned ham is a different process. Those are usually pumped, then set in a brine vat where the ham sits overnight. Then it is smoked."*

Pork made Nodine's famous in gourmet food circles in New York City, where their products are sold in upscale markets like Balducci's, Zabar's, and Dean and DeLuca. Nodine's bacon is made without nitrites, which are suspected of causing cancer. But pork is only part of the smokehouse business.

Ronnie: *"I used to take two boxes of chicken breasts into the market with me, about eighty pounds. It took five years for them to know how to use it and*

to present it. Now we sell more than 2,000 pounds a week."

Nodine's also sells delicious smoked duck breast, turkeys, geese, pheasant, venison sausage, andouille (a spicy Cajun sausage), and salmon smoked just two days after being caught in Norway.

They all end up in the smokehouse, which resembles a giant oven. The smoke is generated by hickory sawdust falling onto a series of hot plates. The warm smoke is fragrant, especially when maple chips or juniper berries are added.

At this custom smokehouse, no job is too big or too small. From a fifteen-hundred-pound buffalo to a three-ounce quail, Nodine's has smoked them all.

Ronnie: "We've smoked everything from bear to venison to raccoon to pheasants. If they bring it in and want to try it, we'll smoke it for them."

Nodine's—it's the smokehouse that made Goshen famous, and it's positively Connecticut. ▪

𝒰PDATE:

Since my first visit, Nodine's outgrew its small processing plant on the family farm and opened a 20,000-square-foot plant 7 miles away in Torrington. The retail shop remains in Goshen, inside a converted dairy barn. Nodine's now distributes its smoked meats, poultry, fish, and cheeses throughout the United States and has developed a large mail-order and gift business. Newer products include Cajun chicken breast, tasso (spicy cured pork used mainly for seasoning), apple-smoked ham, Easter kielbasa, beef jerky, and sweet and hot baby back ribs. Nodine's still does custom smoking orders, including processing game. It's on the Web at www.nodinesmokehouse.com. ▪

SUGAR TIME

You don't have to go to Vermont to get real maple syrup. There are more than twenty-five sugarhouses sprinkled throughout Connecticut, selling syrup and offering a glimpse into our agricultural past.

When it's nearly spring, and nature is beginning to come alive, the cold nights and warmer days of March urge the sap to surge through the sugar maples. Russ Shaller, who taps about 125 trees on his sixty-five acres in Hebron, explains the process from tree to table.

Diane: *"When is a tree ripe for tapping?"*

Russ: *"You should wait until they're fifty years old or 12 inches in diameter for one tap—for two taps, 24 inches."*

Diane (tasting): *"Hmmm, that's not very sweet, just a little, just slightly."*

Russ collects that slightly sweet watery sap and hauls it to his sugarhouse, where his wood-fired evaporator will boil, and boil, and boil it, until it is thick, sugary sweet, and colored like caramel. The evaporator can handle about thirty-two gallons of sap an hour. The thirty-two gallons of sap yield not quite a gallon of syrup.

The sap flows through a series of containers bubbling furiously along the way. Russ traces its path through the evaporator.

Russ: *"The lighter sap will push the heavier syrup through here and then through that hole over there."*

He is looking for the sap to thicken to just the right consistency.

Russ: *"That's not thick enough, so we got some more boiling down to do yet."*

Eventually the syrup is poured off through a series of filters to sift out what's called "sugar sand." As sugar season wears on from February into March, the sap contains less sugar. Russ boils it longer to bring out the flavor, and the syrup turns darker.

Russ: *"The first one is the real light amber, which we get at the beginning of the season. Then at the end of the season it gets darker."*

The real thing tastes dramatically different from most syrup bought at the grocery store, which typically contains only 1 or 2 percent maple.

Russ: *"One of them is actually 14 percent, but ours is 100 percent maple. We just keep boiling it down, and we don't add anything to it."*

Nothing added, nothing needed. It's the real stuff.

Maple syrup time, it's a season that's positively Connecticut. ∎

*M*ORE MAPLE TREATS:

More than half a dozen sugarhouses are fired up each spring in Hebron. If you'd like to tour them, the perfect time is during the Hebron Maple Festival in March. That's when you'll be treated to a lot more than just pancakes and syrup. At sites all over town you'll find tasty treats like maple-cured ham, maple cookies, and maple cotton candy. At Barbara and Selden Wells's place, they drizzle their syrup over snow, a real old-fashioned treat! Hebron celebrated its tenth annual maple festival in March 2000. For dates and locations of future festivals, call the town hall at (860) 228–9312.

For information on visiting sugarhouses elsewhere in the state, send a self-addressed, stamped envelope to: Connecticut Department of Agriculture, 765 Asylum Avenue, Hartford, CT 06105. Write MAPLE SYRUP BROCHURE *on the envelope.* ∎

A TWIST ON TRADITION

North Guilford

Buster Scranton's been boiling sap into syrup in the little red sugarhouse for at least twenty-five years. It's a tradition that has been handed down in the family, but Buster does things a little differently than his father did.

Buster runs about twelve hundred taps, but most of them are not spilling their sap into buckets hanging from the trees. Instead gravity pulls the sap through long tubes of polypropylene, connecting tree to tree and eventually spilling it into stainless-steel cattle troughs. One hundred gallons of sap an hour roils and boils in Buster's pans, yielding about two and one-half gallons of syrup.

Legend has it that the Indians figured out how to make use of maple sap. They would hollow out logs and heat up stones in the fire, using them to extract and thicken the sap into something like syrup. But probably not quite like the rich thick amber liquid that Buster pours out of his wood-fired evaporator.

Buster says that Vermont likes to bill itself as the maple syrup capital, but Connecticut-made syrup stands up just fine. He actually prefers it—his own, anyway. And his favorite way to enjoy it is over vanilla ice cream. Does he ever tire of it? "No—never have, never will." ∎

Artful Living

National Theatre of the Deaf, Hartford

AUTO ARTIST

*M*ost of us look at a car and see a vehicle that will get us to work and take us home. And many of us pass junkyards and see an eyesore. But for one Connecticut man, a rusty old car that someone has discarded is a work of art waiting to happen.

As Peter Tytla leads us deep into the woods off a quiet country road in Salem, he points to a rusty, faded red hulk of a

car. Without wheels, it sits deep in a pile of leaves, overgrown with brush and dusted with snow.

Peter: *"That's a Model-A truck with an International grille on it."*

His long ponytail is streaked with gray now, but Peter can't remember a time when he didn't love cars.

Peter: *"It was an obsession. When I was younger, I used to prowl around places that looked something like this. We used to call them boneyards or junkyards. There was kind of a mystique when you went to these. You saw beautiful old Packards sitting there, and you'd say, 'Gee, I wonder who had that. That was something.'"*

Decades later he's still roaming the boneyards, snapping photos of those old car carcasses. My grandmother used to say "One man's trash is another man's treasure," but for Peter Tytla this is more than trash, more than treasure: It is inspiration for his unique brand of art. Peter meticulously cuts up his junkyard photos and assembles and arranges those fragments on dramatic backgrounds to create fantasy landscapes.

In his East Lyme studio he points to different segments in his collage.

Peter: "This particular gas station comes from Indiana. That one is from Maine. This old lean-to thing is from Connecticut. This car's from Hershey, Pennsylvania. This one's from Massachusetts."

The collages often have themes or tell stories. His work has frequently been featured on the cover of such collector's publications as *Hemming's Almanac*. Peter's originals start at $750 and can go as high as $16,000. Prints sell for less. Some buyers want them personalized, so Peter will insert the image of the customer, often a car buff, into the scene. Although he has been known to feature brand-new Ferraris or Corvettes at a customer's request, Peter prefers antique or classic cars—and the rustier the better.

Peter: "They have more of a feeling for me when they're in that state of decline than when they're all restored. I have more passion for the ones that are still sitting there and haven't been touched in a long time. They have just been left behind, and they were somebody's real pride and joy at one time."

Peter's collages are intricately crafted, involving hundreds and hundreds of applications of cutouts. And he's always striving to do more next time.

Peter: "There's this constant climbing, climbing. It's like the mountain never gives up, it keeps going."

Diane: "What happens if you ever get to the top of the mountain?"

Peter: "I don't know. That's an interesting thought. I'll let you know. I'll give you a call."

If that call ever comes, it's likely to be from a phone in an old car boneyard that's positively Connecticut. ▪

ℳORE:

Before taking up collage making full-time, Peter Tytla directed TV commercials. He has been involved in art one way or another since his infancy. Peter's father, an animator for Disney, drew the baby elephant Dumbo, modeled on the movements of his toddler son. Years later Peter had a vanity license plate that read: IM DUMBO.

Car collectors and enthusiasts may find Peter at an auto show, but if you'd like to see a presentation of his art, contact: Peter Tytla, P.O. Box 43, East Lyme, CT 06333; (860) 739-7105. ▪

MEMORY QUILTS

*T*here are many ways to tell a story—in words, in pictures, on film, and even with fabric. Heather Williams uses all four in the colorful and powerful art form of quilting.

Some people paste their memories into a scrapbook, but not Heather Williams. She stitches the stories of her life into quilts. Heather works with wool, cotton, silks, and sometimes even photographic images screened onto fabric. Her quilts are all about people. One hanging on the wall beside her bed fea-

tures an elderly black man dressed in a suit and jaunty red tie, tipping his hat. His image is surrounded with radiating borders of red ties, stitched onto a quilt backing of men's suiting.

Heather: *"He's a singer from Mississippi. I saw his photograph in* National Geographic *and devoted this to him."*

Some of the quilts are inspired by Heather's favorite women, including authors Alice Walker and Toni Morrison. Another quilt pays homage to Whoopi Goldberg, who is depicted braids and all. Appliqués of the masks of drama and comedy symbolize Whoopi's work as an actress and recall her work with Comic Relief, a program that fights poverty and homelessness.

Some quilts express deep sadness and loss. One mourns a young woman who died in childbirth. Another is Heather's tribute to her mother, who passed away three years ago.

Heather: *"On the back I stitched two birds, which represent my mother and my brother, who had also died."*

Heather was a high-powered attorney in the U.S. Justice Department, prosecuting tough cases of racial violence and police brutality. But while working on legal briefs, she often found herself doodling quilt patterns. She gave up her career in law to return to school. She is now at Yale studying nineteenth-century African-American history. In her free time Heather teaches quilting at the university and at local senior centers.

Heather: *"I feel as a person I am much more integrated now than I used to be. It*

all sort of works, so I'm really happy."

Now Heather's studies find their way into her quilting, where she depicts themes and incidents from African-American history.

Heather: "Right now I am working on my dissertation and a research project. I'm collecting ads that were placed in newspapers after the Civil War by black people looking for family members from whom they'd been separated. So while I am working on that, I am also designing this quilt in my head so that I can work that whole idea into a quilt."

A quilt with a powerful message that's positively Connecticut. ▪

𝒮INCE OUR STORY:

Heather worked with quilters from across Connecticut to create four Freedom Trail quilts. One from each region of the state is on permanent display at the Museum of Connecticut History, located at the State Library, 231 Capitol Avenue, Hartford.

Heather was also involved with quilters from all over the United States in making quilts for the bunks on the freedom schooner Amistad. *Mary Staley at Montgomery College in Maryland organized the project.*

The Farmington Historical Society brought together fifty area quilters to sew a quilt that commemorates the months the Amistad *Africans spent in Farmington in 1841 while funds were raised to send them home, after the Supreme Court decision that freed them. The squares depict some of the places the Africans lived and include a tribute to Foone, the man who despaired of ever going home and drowned himself in the Farmington canal.* ▪

THE CARTOONIST

When I first met my husband, Tom, Guy Gilchrist and his brother Brad were drawing a series of Muppet comic strips in which Miss Piggy was employed as a news anchorwoman. They became our favorite cartoons, and we bought an original through the cartoon syndicate. Years later I found out that Guy lived in Connecticut, and I had the pleasure of finally meeting him.

As the Navigators take the field in Norwich, one fan is looking more at their mascot than at their star hitters. He's cartoonist Guy Gilchrist, who created Tater the Gator for the Navigators, and Rocky for the New Britain Rock Cats. Those characters are emblazoned on most team merchandise.

Guy: "If I can get you to believe that Rocky the Rock Cat is all about rock 'n' roll and baseball and that's New Britain, or that Tater the Gator is sailing down the river in Norwich right up to the stadium and playing ball and that's the Navigators—if I can get you to believe that, you're gonna wear that hat."

Guy Gilchrist knows quite a bit about bringing cartoon characters to life. At the

tender age of twenty-two he was chosen by puppet master Jim Henson to translate the beloved Muppets from TV and movie screens to the funny pages of newspapers all over the world.

Guy: *"No one has to tell you what's going to happen when Kermit tries to break a date with Piggy. You already know, because they're real people."*

Guy breaks into a pretty good impersonation of Kermit's voice: *"'Oh, I'm sorry, Piggy, but I won't be able to go out with you this evening. I have to get a root canal.' You know, then she goes bonkers."*

The Muppets appeared in over 660 daily newspapers from 1981 to 1986. In 1984, President Ronald Reagan and First Lady Nancy Reagan invited Guy to be a guest of honor at the Easter celebration at the White House. Later that week, some of his work was installed as part of the collection at the Smithsonian.

After five years of drawing the Muppets, Guy gave up the strip to concentrate on writing and illustrating children's books based on stories and poems he created for his own children, Lauren and Garrett.

Garrett reads his favorite part from one called "Night Lights and Pillow Fights." The illustrations are of Garrett, in his own room, just the way it looked at the time his dad wrote the book.

Guy has a new challenge. He's taking over the classic comic strip *Nancy*. It's the next step in an career that's positively Connecticut. ∎

𝒰PDATE:

Guy Gilchrist and his brother Brad are still drawing and writing the Nancy *comic strip for nearly four hundred papers around the world. Guy also writes and draws the* Night Lights and Pillow Fights *feature, which started about two years ago and is seen in nearly eighty papers coast to coast. It combines two of Guy's creative pleasures, comic strips and kid's books. Guy has been named Best Book Illustrator several times by the National Cartoonists Society. Brad Gilchrist creates another comic strip,* CT Fan, *which appears in the Sunday* Hartford Courant *sports section. For more on the cartooning brothers, check out www.gilchriststudios.com.* ▪

KEYBOARD VIRTUOSOS

Stonington

*I*n this age of electronic and computer-generated music, a company in Stonington is re-creating instruments from the days of Bach and Beethoven, the instruments that made the music listened to by our Colonial ancestors.

In an old factory building in one of Connecticut's oldest towns, Robert Zapulla is playing a prelude composed for the harpsichord in the 1600s. The harpsichord, an instrument that disappeared for some time, was a predecessor of the piano. Robert is the staff musicologist at Zuckermann Harpsichords International in Stonington, a company that makes early keyboard instruments.

Robert: *"These are based as closely as practical on antiques."*

Zuckermann instruments are reminiscent of historical instruments made in Germany, France, and Italy in the sixteenth and seventeenth centuries. At first glance a harpsichord resembles a piano, but some have white and black keys reversed. Double harpsichords have two keyboards, stacked one atop the other. When a key is pressed, its far end raises a slip of wood, known as a jack. The jack is fitted with a plectrum, which plucks the string on the soundboard. Although modeled on antiques, Zuckermann harpsichords have some updates. For instance, the plectra on early harpsichords were fashioned from crow's feathers.

Robert: *"Today we use plastic instead of crow quill or other types of bird quill."*

Zuckermann is the largest producer of early keyboard instruments in the world. The staff of twelve turns out about three or four instruments a week. Inside the workroom Stuart McCormack is sanding a soundboard. For twenty years Stuart built boats. Now his carpentry is honed to a finer pitch.

Stuart: *"By carving a little wood away on the inside of the case, you can change the sound of the notes."*

The harpsichords fashioned here are more than instruments for making heavenly music. They are exquisitely decorated works of art. One portrays a mythological scene from a medieval painting. Another is elaborately decorated with flowers and birds set against a baroque backdrop of shimmering gold. One instrument took over a year to complete. The artist, Tatyana Nivina, based its decoration on an instrument built in 1733, now housed in a castle in France.

Zuckermann Harpsichords was founded in Greenwich Village in the 1950s, when Wolfgang Zuckermann turned out build-it-yourself harpsichord kits selling for $150.

Robert: *"It was a wildly successful idea, and he sold thousands of them very quickly. He wrote a book called* The Modern Harpsichord, *which was actually some-what controversial. He was critical of the techniques of building modern harpsichords and he took some heat for that."*

In the early 1960s Zuckermann sold the company to David Jacques Way, who moved it to Stonington. Harpsichords made in Stonington can now be found in nearly every country on earth. Zuckermann's also builds other early keyboard instruments, such as clavichords and virginals. And it still sells build-your-own harpsichord kits—but at about $2,000, they cost a bit more than those first sold by Wolfgang Zuckermann. Some buyers build the harpsichords for the challenge of mastering the intricate workmanship. Other buyers are musicians who can't afford a finished instrument, which can sell for as much as $75,000.

In the end they all have a way to make beautiful music that's positively Connecticut. ■

𝒜 FINAL NOTE:

Zuckermann Harpsichords International is open for tours by small groups if you call ahead. You can reach the company at (860) 535–1715. ■

QUEENS OF HEARTS

Madison & Groton

E very little girl grows up hearing that a bride should wear something old, something new, something borrowed, something blue . . .

For Sharon Lepage the something old is her gown. Sharon's mother, Abby, wore it, and so did Abby's best friend in 1962.

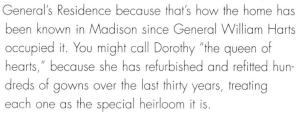

Sharon: *"It really means a lot to me, because my Mom and I are like best friends."*

Abby Lepage: *"I was so touched, I dissolved to tears."*

After more than thirty years in storage the gown had yellowed and stiffened, so they brought it to Dorothy Staley, who understands history and tradition. After all, her shop is set up inside an antique home, which dates to 1729. She calls the shop The

General's Residence because that's how the home has been known in Madison since General William Harts occupied it. You might call Dorothy "the queen of hearts," because she has refurbished and refitted hundreds of gowns over the last thirty years, treating each one as the special heirloom it is.

Dorothy: *"The memories attached to these gowns are the things that money can't buy. I see that young people appreciate more than ever these wonderful family treasures."*

Some of Dorothy's brides wear gowns that have been worn by their mothers, grandmothers, and even great-grandmothers. Some are museum pieces. To Dorothy every dress and every bride is special.

Sharon: *"Dorothy makes you feel like you are the most important person in the world."*

Dorothy mothers each girl, even offering tips on comportment for the big day.

Dorothy: *"Remember as you walk down the aisle, ears to the ceiling! It's really for the photography, so you have fewer shadows on your face."*

Some of her brides become so attached to Dorothy that years after their weddings they still send her photos of their homes and children.

Connecticut has other "queens of hearts" who specialize in refurbishing wedding

gowns. At Sewtique in Groton, Evelyn Kennedy and Barbara Crooks remodel about fifty gowns a year. They say most gowns can be salvaged.

Evelyn: *"We start by seeing how fragile the fabric is. Is the fabric going to break? If the fabric is not durable, no matter what we do it's going to break away. That is true of a lot of netted fabrics, lace fabrics, and some taffeta fabrics. There's no resurrecting that."*

Stains can be a problem, but Evelyn and Barbara have creative techniques for removing or disguising them.

Most gowns need to be made larger, especially the really old ones. One silk brocade gown has been worn three times since it was made in 1880.

Diane: *"A woman of today can't fit into a dress that a woman wore 100 years ago?"*

Evelyn: *"Well, there are some limitations to sizes. But we have made dresses three and even four sizes larger."*

There's more than sentiment behind restoring an old gown. Sometimes it's about value.

One bride brought in the gown her mother wore in 1948. When it was new it probably cost a couple of hundred dollars. To buy a dress of the same quality today you'd pay at least $1,000. Evelyn can restyle the gown for much less.

Repairing, restoring, and wearing heirlooms lends a touch of the past to a wedding that is positively Connecticut. ■

$\mathscr{S}$ INCE OUR STORIES:

More and more of Dorothy's business is designing and creating new gowns. She says because women are getting married later in life, they often know exactly what they want in a gown, and they often cannot find it off the rack.

Evelyn's business has expanded into restoration of other treasured heirlooms, including table and bed linens, lace, tapestries, and quilts. Evelyn often gives workshops on caring for and restoring heirloom textiles to historical societies and other community organizations. ■

RENAISSANCE REVELS

Bristol

*H*ollywood has rediscovered the Elizabethan era, with films like Shakespeare in Love *cleaning up at the 1999 Academy Awards. But for some people in Bristol, a passion for the period is a way of life.*

Scott McNeal's romance with the Renaissance goes back to his high school days. Years later the insurance company employee indulged his love of the period by forming the Renaissance Revels, a sixteenth-century entertainment troupe. We joined them for an afternoon of fencing, rounds singing, and dancing at historic Barnes Chapel in Bristol.

Scott: *"I find it's a stress reliever, because you can be someone else for awhile."*

Someone else such as François del Valois, Duke of Anjou. "He's a French guy," says another player, Gary Gladu. Gary is holding a tall pole, from which long strands of ribbon dangle. The players each hold a strand. As they dance a sixteenth-century version of a maypole dance, the ribbons are intricately woven around the pole.

Gary's wife, Luisa, plays a lady-in-waiting to Queen Elizabeth.

Luisa: *"When we are getting ready for a performance, we get in character the minute we start putting on our costumes. During our rehearsal we are in character.*

Every once in a while we may have to be reminded that it's really 1999."

Performances provide a nice antidote to the daily lives of the players. In real life they have very modern-day careers, including those of computer consultant, systems manager, and training coordinator for a large corporation. When she's not playing Lady Ellie Vator, Kerry Connor teaches respiratory therapy at Manchester Community College.

Kerry: "Let's face it. Every girl wants to grow up and be a princess. So that's what I did. I made myself a princess dress and I loved it."

And while there is a lot of fun and fantasy in the performances, they are based on the troupe's research into the songs, dances, plays, and fashions of the period.

Cheryl McNeal, Scott's wife, describes her attire.

Cheryl: "This is an Elizabethan gown from Queen Elizabeth I. These are actually called queen sleeves. Underneath we have a hoop skirt, and we have a crinoline, and beneath all that, a corset, a boned corset."

The Revels stitch their own costumes, some of which have taken up to a year to complete and are valued at more than $2,000 each.

Kerry: "I think people are looking for an escape from reality. This was a time for chivalry, a time when ladies were ladies and got to wear elegant clothing and men protected them. There really weren't any dragons, but we have this romantic idea that there was evil out there that was clearly defined, and you could fight it, and you could defeat it."

The troupe is available for parties, fairs, fund-raisers, even weddings, and they often march in local parades like the Memorial Day parade in Forestville.

The Renaissance Revels, creating merriment and pageantry that is positively Connecticut. ■

SINCE OUR STORY:

Scott and Cheryl McNeal have started a small business making barrettes, hair combs, headbands, and hats that they sell at Renaissance Faires in New York and Vermont, and at the newest one, in Connecticut. Their programs can be tailored for children or adults (their repertoire includes a few bawdy songs that were popular entertainment in the Middle Ages). Contact them at their Web site: members. xoom.com/Renrevels. ■

TALES FROM THE FIRST WORLD

T*here are many ways to tell a story. Two Connecticut performers incorporate drums and dance into their rich, multicultural, oral tradition.*

With African talking drums and chanting, Jeff and Synia McQuillan are leading the students of Lauralton Hall in Milford on a journey into Africa. Synia begins chanting a traditional West African tale of the trickster spider, called Anansi.

Synia: *"Anansi the spider, Anansi the trickster . . . "*

In their show "Tales from the First World," the McQuillans weave the story of a spider who tricks an elephant in order to feed his family during a famine. Soon the entire audience is on its feet, swaying with the music and echoing Synia's chants.

Synia: *"Why are you standing when you should be dancing? Why are you standing when you should be dancing?"*

The rhythm of Jeff's drumming becomes frantic and so does the dancing. Though this was their first exposure to African storytelling, the students are swept up in the performance.

Jeanell Gadson: *"They got the audience really involved. It was so much fun!"*

Remy Blystone: *"It was amazing! I've never seen so much energy and so much fun put into a performance."*

Jeff and Synia are singers and musicians, too. For more than a decade they have combined their talents in telling stories to children and adults.

Jeff: *"Storytelling like this is multigenerational, it's multicultural. You can go across all kinds of lines with a story and touch everybody."*

Synia: *"Sometimes the only thing our audiences have in common is that they are all gathered there, and with these images they can all travel together. And it can be a good journey. It can be a joyful journey."*

Their tales are from Africa, the Caribbean, and here at home. Jeff collects his tales

from all over.

Jeff: *"I like sitting down in kitchens with old people and spending time and just listening to them."*

Jeff and Synia are Connecticut's 1998 state troubadours appointed by the Connecticut Commission on the Arts. Their style is a bit of a departure from their predecessors in the honorary post, many of whom were folk musicians.

Synia: *"Troubadour to me is oral tradition, whether it's through song or through storytelling."*

They incorporate Connecticut history into their songs and stories, too.

Synia: *"That helps keep the history alive. Then it lives, then it breathes, then it can never die."*

Seated side by side on their living room sofa in New Haven, as Jeff strums his guitar, they begin to sing a song Jeff wrote. The song is inspired by the Indian word for Connecticut, which means long river.

Jeff: *"From Portland down to Haddam's Neck, the memory's like an old shipwreck. Even though the body's gone, the river hums a gospel song."*

Synia joins in on the chorus.

Jeff and Synia: *"Long long river, what do you see, long long river, tell me what you know."*

A song that's positively Connecticut. ◼

ƧINCE OUR STORY:

Synia is teaching Spanish full time at New Haven's High School in the Community. Jeff teaches at the Education Center for the Arts and Foster School in Hamden. They record on the American Melody label, founded by another Connecticut troubadour, Phil Rosenthal. To find out more, or hire them for a performance or workshop, visit their Web site at first world.bizland.com.

To find out more about the traditions of storytelling, or to attend a storytelling event, contact the Connecticut Storytelling Center, located at Connecticut College in New London at (860) 439–2764. ◼

LOUDER THAN WORDS

A udiences around the world have enjoyed a unique theatrical experience, seeing a stage play in an entirely new way, because of a theater company that is positively Connecticut.

The *Odyssey* has been told and retold for twenty-seven centuries, but never quite like this. The classic tale is being translated and narrated in two languages simultaneously—English and American Sign Language.

It is the season-opening production for the National Theatre of the Deaf.

Marcia Tilchen is one of only two hearing actors in the cast. She finds it a challenge.

Marcia: *"You have to find a balance between doing a good job voicing for the deaf nonspeaking actors, and at the same time trying to do your own acting work."*

Willie Connelly, a deaf actor, plays the role of the great adventurer Odysseus. He speaks to us about his role, comically implying that he's less than an appropriate choice physically. He signs as he speaks.

Willie: *"In the* Odyssey, *Odysseus is a big, muscular hero. And here I am—Joe Average!"*

All summer the cast has worked on expressing the text through sign language in a way that not only carries the performance but also raises it to another level of experience.

Will Rhys is the artistic director of the Tony award–winning company. He explained a little about how these actors are different—more comfortable using expressive gesture.

Will: *"We seem to be stifled by our own bodies, but these actors are free physically."*

And the audiences, he says, love the visual dimension of sign and the physical freedom the actors bring to their roles.

Will: *"They see that sign language is not English transplanted word for word. It's a language unto itself, and it looks wonderful. It's so beautiful to look at."*

The National Theatre of the Deaf is the longest continually touring theater group in the world. In the first twenty-two years of its existence, the company visited twenty-six countries. In some of those countries the company has helped start up similar troupes.

In the early days of the National Theatre of the Deaf, it was difficult to attract audiences. Today the company is world renowned. Still, David Hays, who founded the company in 1967, wonders about its future.

David: *"These days the future is survival. We just have to keep alive."*

For now, though, the National Theatre of the Deaf is alive and well and a treasure that is positively Connecticut. ■

$\mathcal{M}$ORE:

Founding artistic director David Hays left the National Theatre of the Deaf about three years ago. The company now has a new home and a new focus. In July 2000 it moved to Hartford, having outgrown its space in Chester. And rather than touring continually, NTD is now establishing a resident repertory company that will perform at theaters across Connecticut. A second company, The Little Theatre of the Deaf, performs plays for children. NTD is soon to release a CD of its acclaimed production of "The Christmas That Almost Wasn't," based on the poem by Ogden Nash and narrated by John Lithgow. ■

CONNECTICUT'S TROPICS

L ogee's Greenhouses Ltd. is an enchanted world of flowering and fragrant tropical, subtropical, and garden plants. It is the exclusive source for some heirloom and newly introduced plants.

When we visited Logee's, the calendar still said winter, but Byron Martin, whose family has run the business for more than a century, felt otherwise.

Byron: "In the greenhouse it's springtime. The light levels have increased, the sun is rising in the sky, and the warm temperatures as well as the length of day have wakened up many of the plants."

And it's not just spring, it's spring in the tropics. Around here they like to say, "Why spend your money on airfare when you can drive to Logee's Greenhouses and visit a tropical rain forest?" Step inside and your nose will tell you these gardeners specialize in growing things that smell really good, from the tiny blooms on the jasmine to the footlong flowers of the angel's trumpet.

Byron: "They're very fragrant at night. In fact the scent in the greenhouse is almost intoxicating."

Byron's mother, Joy Logee Martin, has worked in the greenhouse nearly all of her eighty-seven years. She took over the business from her father. Joy lovingly points out his century-old Ponderosa lemon tree, with lemons as fat as grapefruits.

Joy: "It was delivered by horse and wagon. My brothers told me how they danced around while Papa opened this great big box."

Tomatoes grow on trees here too, and coffee beans and kumquats. Since 1892 the Logee-Martin family has sold plants for greenhouse and indoor-container gardening. Customers all over the world seek out the 1,500 varieties of rare and unusual plants. In the tissue culture lab and in the greenhouses, Byron is creating new varieties.

Byron: *"I think some of the best things I have done were those stabs in the dark, where all of a sudden they appeared. When I tried to think about it in a logical way, it was often mundane."*

Indoor gardening is a growing hobby, Byron says, and it differs from outdoor gardening in subtle ways.

Byron: *"A relationship develops between you and the plant. You have to water it every day, you watch every leaf unfold. You watch the blossoms in a much more intimate way—certainly in a more intense way—than you ever do in your garden."*

At Logee's Greenhouses in Danielson the growing season is year-round, and it's positively Connecticut. ■

*M*ORE:

Logee's is at 141 North Street in Danielson. ■

A GARDENER'S PARADISE
Litchfield

Another must for gardeners: a visit to White Flower Farm on Route 63 in Litchfield. Its world-renowned catalog comes to life on White Flower's seventy-two acres, ten of which are devoted to test and display gardens. My favorite is the iris garden, where new and old varieties are tested and combine to create a spectacular display.

White Flower Farm was founded in 1950 by William Harris, an editor at *Fortune* magazine, and his wife, Jane Grant, a writer for the *New York Times*. They issued their catalog under the pen name Amos Pettingill. "Amos" still tends the gardens and writes the catalog, but these days he is really Eliot Wadsworth, who bought the farm from Harris in 1976. Hardy perennial flowers, bulbs, and shrubs are their specialty, but the catalog now includes annuals, vines, and trellises, as well as plants and seeds for the kitchen garden. The retail store and the gardens are open to visitors daily, April through October. ■

BEAUTY INSIDE AND OUT

T*he views from the country estate known as Hill-Stead are spectacu-lar—the rolling fields and woodlands of the upper Farmington Valley, and off to the west the Litchfield Hills. But the views indoors are even more amazing.*

The Hill-Stead mansion, now a National Historic Landmark, was built in 1901 on 152 parklike acres as the home of Alfred and Ada Pope. It now houses a museum. Ruth Appelhoff is the curator.

Ruth: *"The Popes were from Cleveland and made all their money there. When they retired here, they were actually gentlemen farmers."*

The house was designed to showcase the Popes' exceptional collection of Impressionist art by Degas, Manet, Monet, and Cassatt.

Ruth: *"These paintings were purchased by the Popes almost immediately after they were painted. We like to say that the paint was hardly dry!"*

The Colonial Revival–style home was designed by one of America's first prominent female architects, who happened to be the Popes' daughter Theodate, a graduate of nearby Miss Porter's School. With the assistance of the well-known architectural firm of McKim, Mead, and White, Theodate created a home where the sweep of the drawing room pulls the eye from one Monet masterpiece to another. The sunny yellow morning room frames an earlier work by Monet.

By all accounts Theodate was an interesting and unusual woman for her time. Highly educated and highly independent, she made her mark in architecture—and in agriculture, too. Dairymen traveled to Hill-Stead to see the prize-winning cows Theodate raised. She remained single well into her forties, but

she took in three boys whom she raised as her own. In 1915 she was onboard the *Lusitania*, heading for a psychic research conference in England, when the ocean liner was sunk by a German U-boat. Theodate floated unconscious in the water for hours before being rescued.

After her parents' death, Theodate lived at Hill-Stead with her husband, John Wallace Riddle, a career diplomat whom she married when she was forty-eight. Their home was a social center, as it had been when Alfred and Ada were living.

Ruth: *"They invited people from all over the world to come visit them—writers, politicians, painters, and musicians."*

Henry James, Sinclair Lewis, Thornton Wilder, Mary Cassatt, and Eleanor Roosevelt were among their guests, according to museum spokeswoman Margy Foulk.

Margy: *"It was common for people of their station in life to entertain with musicals, speakers, and poetry readings."*

They entertained not only in beautiful art-filled rooms, but in a sunken garden that might have inspired the Impressionists they so admired.

After Theodate Pope Riddle's death in 1946, Hill-Stead became a museum, with its Impressionist art collection, Chinese porcelains, and original furnishings intact. Today it is maintained much as it was when Theodate lived here.

The Hill-Stead Museum, the legacy of a talented woman who was positively Connecticut. ■

P.S.

Hill-Stead is open for tours Tuesday through Sunday at 10:00 A.M.; the last tour begins at 4:00 P.M. For information call (860) 677–9064, or visit www.hillstead.org. ■

IN THE GARDEN:

The year 2001 marks the one-hundredth anniversary of the house and the tenth anniversary of the popular Sunken Garden Poetry Festival at the Hill-Stead Museum, cosponsored by the museum and *Northeast* magazine. The six performances start in June and run through mid-August. Readings have been known to draw as many as 3,500 people to the grounds. For details call (860) 677–9064.

Historic People
and Places

New London Harbor Light

THE FREEDOM SCHOONER

*A*fter covering the Amistad *story for fifteen years—through the erection of a monument, the completion of a freedom trail, and the release of a Steven Spielberg film—I knew I had to be there when they launched a replica of the schooner. What I observed that March morning in Mystic is the power of a dream realized. The new ship's cargo is history, and her sails are powered by memory.*

Warren Marr steps onto the dock beside the *Amistad*. His job is to break the chains that bind the 129-foot schooner to land. The old man needs a little help from a friend to swing the sledgehammer that smashes the links. That seems right, since fulfilling Marr's dream of building the ship took a little help from

many friends. And it's fitting because the *Amistad* story itself is a lesson from history about what people of goodwill, working together, can accomplish.

The story begins in 1839, when fifty-three men, women, and children were snatched from their homeland (now Sierra Leone) in Africa and held captive on board the original ship *La Amistad*, headed for Cuba and slavery. Before they landed, the captives mutinied. Their leader, Sengbe Pieh (also known as Cinque), killed the captain of the Spanish ship and tried to force its crew to take the Africans home. Instead the ship wandered a zigzag course, eventually landing near Montauk, Long Island. The Africans were arrested, brought to New London, and jailed in New Haven where they fought for two years for their freedom and their right to go home.

People from throughout Connecticut supported their battle through a series of trials. In 1841 John Quincy Adams, by then a former president, won their liberty in the Supreme Court. It was a landmark case in civil and human rights.

Warren Marr knew the story and dreamed of the ship's re-creation for twenty years. George Bellinger knew the *Amistad* story, too. In his steward-ship of the Afro-American Historical Society in New Haven, he came to see it as the most important civil rights tale in the state's history. He fought first for a monument commemorating the Africans, which stands today outside New Haven City Hall. Then George joined forces with Warren and Mystic Seaport to build the ship as a floating tribute to freedom.

Two hundred and forty people worked for two years at the Mystic Seaport Restoration Shipyard, using historic techniques and tools to construct the $3.1 million replica of the *Amistad*.

On a cool morning in March 2000, George smiles down upon 10,000 peo-ple—including dignitaries from across the state, from Washington, D.C., and from Sierra Leone—who are gathered at Mystic Seaport to witness the launch of the replica schooner.

George Bellinger (speaking to the crowd): *"This is a day to feel gleeful and solemn, proud and hum-bled. Most of all today I know that dreams do come true."*

Connecticut contributed $2.5 million to help create what U.S. Senator Christopher Dodd calls *"an extraordinary gift to your fellow citizens."* He dedi-cates the new *Amistad* to a mission of reconciliation.

Senator Chris Dodd: *"Today the* Amistad *story moves beyond the page into timbers, sail, and line. From this day forward she will show the world that evil must not have the last word."*

The *Amistad* launch is more than a history lesson, though. It is a story with a human face, and that face is Samuel Pieh's. Samuel is the great-grandson of Sengbe Pieh, the man who led the Africans' ship-board revolt and eventual return to Africa. Now an

American, Samuel beams as he and his family watch the *Amistad* come alive.

As we walk toward the dock for the christening, I ask him what this day means to him.

Samuel Pieh: *"This is a red letter day in all our lives. It's proof that common people make history every day."*

The ceremony is punctuated with African drumming and colored with emotion. The ship's bell is rung fifty-three times, once for each of the original African captives. Then actress Ruby Dee cracks the ship's bow with a bottle—filled not with champagne but with water from Sierra Leone, Cuba, and Long Island Sound.

Amistad Captain Bill Pinkney sees the creation of the ship as the dream of a lifetime.

Captain Pinkney: *"This is 'The Great Adventure' I have been pursuing since childhood."*

For him, the adventure commences on the ship's maiden voyage to New York Harbor in time for Independence Day 2000.

As the christening comes to an end, children release a flock of white doves into the sky; an armada of sailboats, yachts, canoes, and kayaks blow air horns and whistles; and the tall ships HMS *Rose* and *Mystic Whaler* shoot their cannons in tribute. The crowds gathered on the riverbank and in the Seaport cheer. Some people wipe away tears.

Like Sengbe Pieh and his fellow Africans more than 160 years ago, Warren Marr and George Bellinger have achieved their dream, with a little help from their friends. The *Amistad* is a dream come true that is positively Connecticut. ∎

*𝒰*PDATE:

Amistad's maiden voyage took her to New York City's harbor on Independence Day for OpSail 2000, and then to New London harbor. Her home port is New Haven, but she will roam the world as a messenger of freedom and racial harmony.

SETTING SAIL

Mystic

If you'd like to sail Long Island Sound in an old-time craft, you can enjoy salt air, sea, and some positively Connecticut history aboard the *Mystic Whaler*, a replica of the ships that plied the seas during the whaling era. The 100-foot-long schooner was completely refurbished in 1995, refitted from the hull up when Captain John Eginton and his wife, Marelda, bought the boat.

The schooner sails from Memorial Day weekend through mid-October and offers day cruises; lobster dinner cruises; two-, three-, and five-day overnights (which may take in Block Island or Sag Harbor); and theme trips such as the three-day Lighthouse Cruise, the Sea Music Cruise, Art under Sail, and the Pirate Cruise, the latter described as three days of high jinks in a search for booty. Accommodations range from private cabins to a bunk in the great room. For more information call the *Mystic Whaler* in Mystic or look them up at www.mysticwhaler.com.

KEEPERS OF THE FLAME

Stonington, New London, Noank, Stratford & Norwalk

A mong the most popular travel destinations in Connecticut are the many lighthouses that mark our shoreline. Although more sophisticated navigational aids have decreased the need for these structures, the passion for them is growing. And for some people, a peek isn't enough—they want to be part of preserving the maritime past that's positively Connecticut.

Captain John Wadsworth grew up on Long Island Sound, taking over his father's sportfishing business in Waterford. His

boat, the *Sunbeam Express*, once carried roughnecks to and from oil rigs. These days the destinations are often the dozen lighthouses at the eastern end of the Sound.

Captain John: *"There are people that keep a log book and log every lighthouse that they've seen and take pictures of 'em. They get together and swap stories. It's quite a little lighthouse society."*

Local historian Ben Rathbun is often on board as tour guide. At New London harbor he points out Pequot, the oldest lighthouse, first built in 1760, when Colonial America had only three others.

Ben: *"The first light was built by the proceeds from the lottery that they'd held. Apparently they bid it out to the lowest bidder, because shortly after they built it a huge crack developed."*

The tour also takes in the light marking Lattimer's Reef, which is just a cast-iron column on a stony base.

Ben: *"The first keeper here spent twenty-four years in that little bit of a 24-foot-diameter lighthouse. It was like living in a silo. If it was a job, nobody would take it today, but it was customary in those days. People went away on three-year whaling voyages then, too. It was a different lifestyle and way of thinking."*

Apparently the new owner of the lighthouse on North Dumpling Island has a grander view of the life of the light keeper. The decommissioned lighthouse is now a vacation home complete with windmill.

Captain John: *"As I understand it, he was told to take the windmill down because he didn't have a permit. He said, 'I'm Lord Dumpling, this is my island, my domain, and if you want it, you come take it,' and it's still there!"*

Ben thinks the increased interest in lighthouses comes from knowing that we'll never see their likes again.

Ben: *"Every time one is destroyed, they put up an ugly utilitarian structure because of the dollars involved."*

There has never been another lighthouse like the one built in 1909 on New London Ledge. I'd sailed by it many times and had always wanted to look inside. A Cross Sound Ferry tugboat took us out there, with Jerry Olsen as our guide. The Coast Guard maintains the automated signal light, but Jerry's New London Ledge Lighthouse Foundation has a long-term lease on the lighthouse and is restoring the French Empire–style mansion. No one lives there now, unless you count Ernie, said to be the ghost of a former lighthouse keeper.

Jerry: *"Ernie was despondent after his wife was supposed to have gone off with a ferry captain. He went up to the top of the lighthouse and jumped off."*

Jerry claims to have encountered another spirit while he was deep inside a basement cistern.

Jerry: *"It sounded like a woman clearing her throat. No noise penetrates these walls, because the walls are 8 feet thick. And there is a story of a 1913 capsizing of a sailboat out here in the Sound where a woman was lost."*

Jerry hopes one day to rent the lighthouse to an artist or writer looking for solitude and inspiration.

While boats are the only traffic around New London Ledge, the Stonington Lighthouse sits right at the end of the main road through the village. The lighthouse was moved to this spot after it was threatened by erosion. When the Coast Guard replaced it with another beacon, the lighthouse became a museum showcasing Stonington's 350-year history. Curator Louise Pittaway tells us that for much of the last half of the nineteenth century, when Stonington was a railroad hub between Boston and New York, the harbor was clogged with passenger steamboats, seal hunters, whalers, coastal traders, and the commercial fishing fleet.

Louise: *"The lighthouse keeper had to think of all this. The water was really the main street in those days, so you had to think of all this activity going in and out of the harbor."*

The Stonington lighthouse was decommissioned before the turn of the last century, but there are still twenty-two working lights in Long Island Sound, and Chief Warrant Officer John Strauser is the Coast Guard officer in charge of all of them. The only manned lighthouse left in the United States is in Boston, but the Stratford Point Lighthouse comes pretty close. John and his family live there.

Since the signal is automated, Officer Strauser is technically not the lighthouse keeper, but he has reminders of their heavy responsibilities, including the magnificent lamp that guided ships for one hundred years.

John: *"Augustin Jean Fresnel was a French physicist. He came up with this principle of progressive prisms to a central dish so you were able to project a column of light."*

In 1969 new lights replaced the historic Fresnel lens, but they were too big for the

cupola, so the cupola was removed and trucked to Stratford's Booth Memorial Park, where it stayed for twenty years. In 1990 the cupola was reattached to the lighthouse, restoring its original look. Although the lighthouse is not officially open to the public, John enjoys showing it to lighthouse lovers who drop by.

John: *"Lighthouses have always been a symbol of faith, a symbol of safe haven. I think people find it very comforting to see a lighthouse."*

In Norwalk, the Sheffield Island Lighthouse looks a bit like an old stone church. It is the second light on the spot, erected in 1868. At various times in its history Sheffield Island was home to a dairy farm, a glamorous resort (in the 1930s), a rumrunner's paradise (during Prohibition), and, reputedly, a hippie commune (in the 1970s). Now it's the home of the Stewart McKinney Wildlife Refuge, populated mostly by deer and birds.

Devoted lighthouse supporters Pauline and Mark Shlegel love to share the local legends.

Mark: *"Some of the little islands out here are known as 'the cows.' The reason for that is at low tide the cows would wander out and get stranded by the tide, so the farmers would have to go out with a rowboat and milk the cows."*

After the turn of the twentieth century, other lighthouses took its place, and Sheffield became a summer home for a Norwalk family. In 1987 the nonprofit Seaport Association bought the lighthouse. Since then it has gotten a new roof, the tower has been restored, and the grounds improved. Much of that work has been carried out by volunteers.

Pauline: *"We want this here for our grandkids. This is history that we can't get back. Too many lighthouses have fallen to ruin and no one has cared."*

A ferry from the seaport unloads passengers several times each day, and there are guided tours for visitors. The island is a popular place for weddings and parties, and

there are weekly clambakes in season. Late in the evening, when the last clambake guests have boarded the ferry, the only person left on the island is Matt DeVito, the caretaker.

Matt: *"You have to be comfortable with being all alone on an island. You either love it or you hate it. Right now I'm loving it."*

In Noank, Jason Pilalas salutes passing boats with a shot from the cannon mounted outside his lighthouse home at Morgan Point. And if it seems as if he's having an awful lot of fun, it may be because he's living out his boyhood fantasy.

Jason: *"When I was ten years old and living in Greenwich, I used to row out to Great Captain's Island, where the exact twin of this lighthouse resides, and talk to the Coast Guardsmen and dream of owning it. Of course that could never be, but boys do dream."*

Forty years later Jason, who had long since moved to California, saw an ad in the *Wall Street Journal*. The Morgan Point lighthouse, just like the one from his childhood, was for sale. It took about $1 million to turn it into a special family home, including building a replica of the missing light room.

Jason: *"Opinion is divided about whether it was the hurricane of '38 or Coast Guard frugality that removed it when the lighthouse was decommissioned. But we felt that you can't have a lighthouse without a light room, and it would be a spectacular place to sit and enjoy cocktails or sunrise or sunset or fireworks or thunderstorms."*

And Morgan Point is the perfect setting for a remarkable collection of nautical antiques, collected by this Navy veteran, who saw two tours of duty in Vietnam on the USS *Sutherland*.

Although Morgan Point is now a private home, Jason recognizes that the lighthouse is a local landmark and that he is a caretaker of history.

Jason: *"I had to own it. I wanted to own it when I was ten, and I wanted to own it when I was fifty. Sometimes dreams do come true, and this one has for me."*

You might call Jason and the others modern-day lighthouse keepers. Even in lighthouses that are automated or no longer needed, there are still people who care for them, making sure these beacons shining from our past do not go out. They are keepers of the flame who are positively Connecticut. ∎

More:

The Sunbeam Fleet in Waterford offers regular lighthouse sightseeing cruises; call (860) 443–7259 for details. To take a summertime tour of New London Ledge Lighthouse, contact Project Oceanology at (860) 445–9007. To visit the Sheffield Island Lighthouse and receive information about ferry schedules and clambakes, contact the Norwalk Seaport Association at (203) 838–9444.

THE CRYPT

A crypt in the basement of Center Church on the green in New Haven contains more than a hundred old headstones. How the crypt came to be, and how it is being restored, makes for quite a story.

Bill Murray heads the preservation committee at Center Church.

Bill: *"In 1812 the church decided that it wanted to put a new church building, our fourth meeting house, up on this particular spot. In order to do that they would have to build it over a portion of the original Colonial burial ground. They finally got permission to do it with the understanding that they would take care of the crypt."*

Now the church has hired specialists from the University of Pennsylvania to restore the crypt and its headstones.

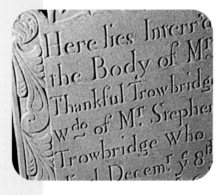

You might wonder why headstones that have been preserved indoors for more than 180 years would need restoration, but it's not what's coming from the sky that's wearing them down, but what's coming up from below. That's why the first step in the restoration is replacing the floor. The cement floor that was installed in 1879 sealed in underground moisture. The only escape route was through the headstones, which acted as wicks for water and salts.

Bill: *"It's actually drawing up the salts from the bodies, and if you touch this headstone, really you're probably touching, in a way, the remains of the early settlers of this colony."*

The new brick floor allows moisture to evaporate into the air.

The other big task is cleaning the headstones, some of which are three hundred years old. Elizabeth Bede is applying a special poultice.

Elizabeth: *"You put it on, the solvent leeches into the stone, and then as the material dries it draws it out. It draws the soiling and the salts and the solvent back out of the stone."*

The idea is to stabilize the stones and stop the erosion. Some need painstaking repairs. Joel Snodgrass is fashioning a new base for one.

Joel: *"It's a pinning system. In this case we're using stainless steel pins because it's noncorrosive. And what we'll do is pour a rough form around the stone with a compatible mix that we've formulated and once that sets, then we can come back and do our final tooling on it."*

Murray's committee has worked hard to raise the money needed for the restoration.

Bill: *"These people who came here to America in those early days, with their determination and their struggle, in order to establish a new world and a place where they could live in freedom and better conditions, had to sacrifice a great deal to come here. And it sort of stands as a model for us in the future."*

Diane (to Joel): *"How long do you think these stones can last with the kind of care they're getting now?"*

Joel: *"I always like to think forever, but really the only thing you can do in preservation is buy more time."*

More time that's positively Connecticut. ■

SINCE OUR STORY:

At least $250,000 has been raised to restore and preserve the crypt, the resting place of so many early luminaries of New Haven. Recently a plaque commemorating Theophilus Eaton was placed in the crypt. He was governor of the colony from about 1638 to 1657. Other notables who are buried there include Benedict Arnold's first wife, the grandparents of U.S. President Rutherford B. Hayes, and one of the founders of Yale University, James Pierpont. The crypt is open for tours three days a week from April through November. ■

A MERRY MUSEUM

T he year 2000 marked the tenth anniversary of the New England Carousel Museum in Bristol, a colorful place that appeals to the child in all of us.

Children and carousels—they just seem to go together. Not necessarily, says Louise DeMars, executive director of the New England Carousel Museum.

Louise: "Seniors love the carousel—they grew up with it as their entertainment. Adults adore it. They remember their early days riding the carousel. It's the children today who don't have a lot of carousel experience. They're busy being bombarded with video games."

But at the New England Carousel Museum in Bristol, children have a chance to enjoy what was first meant to entertain adults. In the late 1800s in this country, carousels were installed in beer gardens and taverns. Trolley companies placed them in parks located at the end of the line, to lure extra passengers and increase ridership. Some folks still remember those days.

Louise: "We've had people come in and pull up a park bench and just sit for hours staring at the horses and remembering the days of their youth when they rode the carousel."

The invention of the carousel has been traced back to A.D. 500, when carousels were used as training devices to help noblemen sharpen their jousting skills and prepare for war.

Some other things you'll learn at the museum: Most carousel horses are decorated on only one side; the animals on the inside rings are smaller; and there are three types of horses on carousels—standers, prancers, and jumpers. Carousel horses are quite collectible these days, both for nostalgia and as art.

Louise: "There are three schools of carving in the United States. The Coney Island style, the country fair style, and the Philadelphia style. Just as you can walk into an art museum and tell the difference between a Monet and a van Gogh, you can do the same with carousel art."

The Coney Island style of carving is the glitziest. The horses are painted with twenty-three-karat gold and encrusted with cut glass "jewels."

The Bristol museum nurtures its own carving school, featuring artists like Juan Andreu from Valencia, Spain, who was creating a wondrous steed as we watched.

Juan: *"It takes about three pieces of wood to make the head. Then the body is one piece for the top and another piece for the bottom, with a hollow center."*

Juan restores antique animals and carves new ones. Inspired by Connecticut's maritime history, he created three with an ocean theme: a manatee, a dolphin, and a sea otter.

Louise DeMars has helped shape the museum for more than eight years. She says this is a joyful place.

Louise: *"Most people have a smile put on their face when they ride a merry-go-round, and these exhibits make them feel that way, too."*

Some day Louise hopes to develop a carousel conservation center at the museum, to preserve Connecticut's historic carousels and educate the next generation of carousel lovers, who are positively Connecticut. ■

*M*ORE:

The New England Carousel Museum, at 95 Riverside Avenue, is located in a former "stockingette," a factory where stockings were made at the turn of the century. The museum can be rented for special events, including sleepover parties for children. For information call (860) 585–5411.

The museum is drawing up a Carousel Trail, a map linking thirteen sites around the state that have carousels or related displays.

Plans call for a museum of Bristol fire history to move into the building and for a cultural center that will include a fine art gallery and space for art classes.

ART FARM

Wilton

I t's the only national park in Connecticut, and it is a most unusual one. Weir Farm National Historic Site is the only national park dedicated to American painting.

The farm in Wilton inspired one of the most important artists in the American Impressionist movement—J. Alden Weir. Weir is said to have bought the farm in exchange for a still life painting he had just purchased. The farm became a second home to Weir and other Impressionists, including Childe Hassam, Albert Pinkham Ryder, and Henry Twachtman. Now a National Historic Site, the farm's woodlands, pond, orchards, and stone walls inspire new generations of artists who work in its studios. Visitors wander the trails that crisscross the property and, with a special brochure in hand, see the sites that inspired some of Weir's paintings.

Although the paintings are not displayed at the farm, at a show at the Lyme Academy of Fine Arts I had the rare opportunity to view Weir's work through the eyes of the artist's granddaughter, Anna Smith. Looking at this special collection of paintings still owned by Weir's family is a little like leafing through an extraordinary and exquisite family scrapbook.

Anna discusses a painting of a seated woman watching her child perched on a stool. The child is gazing out a window.

Anna: *"The little girl is my mother in their apartment on Twelfth Street in New York. That's my grandmother Anna and that's Gyp, their dog. I own this little stool and this chair."*

You can imagine how dear these paintings are to his descendants, since many feature Weir's wife and children. Anna and I look at a painting of two placid and beautifully dressed girls riding donkeys.

Anna: *"The donkeys were named Tommy and Pacer, and my Aunt Dorothy was terrified of them. I think that Aunt Cora had to pose for both of them, then he just changed the face a little bit."*

There's her grandmother's farm.

Anna: *"I love this picture. It feels as if you could just keep going back walking into those nice sunny glades. I know the place well. I used to go every summer to stay with my grandmother for two weeks. I loved that place."*

And there's a painting of her grandfather's dog, Bush.

Anna: *"Isn't that a great painting of a dog? I can almost smell him!"*

The Christmas Tree, which may be Weir's best-known work, features Anna's mother as a woeful-looking girl clutching a porcelain-head doll.

Anna: *"She absolutely hated having her portrait painted, especially then as a little girl when she wanted to play with her new doll."*

Weir helped lead a group of artists, known as The Ten American Painters, who created their own version of Impressionism and their own way of portraying the American countryside. Their influence would change art in this country forever. At Weir Farm National Historic Site the landscape that meant so much to them, and now to us, is preserved as a place that's positively Connecticut. ▪

---

*M*ORE:

Weir's sixty-acre farm on Nod Hill Road in Wilton was threatened by suburban development in the 1980s, but by 1988 the Trust for Public Land helped reassemble the original farm property.

Working with the National Trust for Historic Preservation, the Connecticut Trust for Historic Preservation, the Weir Farm Trust, and the State of Connecticut, the land was preserved for public use and designated as a National Historic Site.

In March 2000 the National Park Service announced the acquisition of another seven and one-half acres, which means the park service can move forward with plans for a new museum-quality gallery to showcase paintings by Weir and the others who painted at the farm. The grounds are open daily from dawn to dusk. For information on studio tours and special events, call (203) 834–1896 or check out the Web site www.nps.gov/wefa. ▪

STEAM ENGINE CIDER MILL

N *othing says autumn like a cold glass of cider, and in Connecticut it's hard to find cider better than the one pressed at B. F. Clyde Cider Mill in Old Mystic, which just may be the only steam-powered mill in New England.*

The sound of a steam whistle has accompanied the making of cider at B. F. Clyde's for almost a century. Jack Bucklyn, the man in charge, wears a striped engineer's hat.

Jack: *"This is the steam boiler that provides the steam. The steam travels through the steam pipe, over to the steam engine itself. And that's a fifteen-horsepower steam engine, and it's ninety-two years old. It provides all the power to run everything in the mill."*

Jack Bucklyn's a Connecticut Yankee who took over the family mill started by B. F. Clyde.

Jack: *"That was my grandfather, Benjamin F., and you can guess what that was—Benjamin Franklin. Naturally."*

Diane: *"That's about as American as it gets."*

Jack: *"Yep."*

It's still a family operation with Jack's wife, daughters, and granddaughters working behind the counter, his grandson loading the apples into the press, and his son-in-law Harold Miner helping make the cider.

Jack: *"That's how I acquired most of my son-in-laws."*

Diane: *"How do you mean? They came to work for you and then met your girls?"*

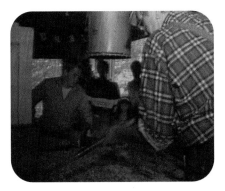

Jack: "No. When my girls got to be about fourteen, this seemed to be one of the most popular places in the fall. You know, the boys came around, and I never lacked for help that way."

The customers who gather round to watch the fragrant juice squeezed from the apples seem like family, too. White-haired Ken MacGregor of Mystic says he's been drinking the cider from Clyde's since he was about ten years old.

Diane: "More or less raised on this stuff?"

Ken: "Yep, can't do without this."

One of the reasons the cider is so good is that it's fresh. Sometimes it barely makes it from the press to the cooler before customers are bottling it and buying it. These days all the juice is pasteurized for extra safety. And if you're over twenty-one, there's hard cider, popular here since Prohibition.

B. F. Clyde's Cider Mill, a remnant of the past that's positively Connecticut. ■

ℐINCE OUR STORY:

Turning one-hundred years old doesn't mean you can't keep up with the times. B. F. Clyde's is now a winery, too. To celebrate its centennial season, B. F. Clyde's produced its first sparkling cider champagne. It was so popular it's now trying apple raspberry sparkling cider champagne, too. These days the hard cider packs a bit more kick and is sold in wine bottles instead of plastic jugs.

Clyde's is open from July through December. They've opened a bakery, turning out—you guessed it—delicious apple pies, apple turnovers, and cider doughnuts. You'll find Clyde's at 129 North Stonington Road in Old Mystic. ■

HANDS-ON HISTORY

*A*t Dudley Farm in North Guilford, they grow more than vegetables. They grow knowledge. The farm is an outdoor classroom for school-children.

On an early spring day, a yellow school bus pulls up to Dudley Farm, and laughing, excited kids jump off. They cluster around Tom Leddy as he demonstrates a one-hundred-year-old farm tool for planting and guides a young boy in the technique.

Tom: *"Don't push down too hard. Just push forward."*

These third-graders are learning how farm children a century ago would have helped till the soil and plant crops. Tom Leddy and Jim Powers are the teachers who bring that simpler past to life for students from Guilford and other Connecticut towns.

Third grader Katylinn Castolene: *"It would have been hard work, but it would have been kind of fun."*

The Dudleys were among the first settlers in Guilford, arriving in 1639. They worked this land for nearly 300 years. David Dudley was part of the tenth generation to live on the land. When he died in 1991, he donated the farm to the local volunteer fire company.

Jim: *"Like many of us, the fire department members lament changes that have taken place in our society. They wanted to have a place representative of a simpler and maybe kinder past."*

So they established the Dudley Foundation to maintain and operate the farm as a historical, educational, and recreational resource.

Tom: *"We can re-create things an awful lot better here than trying to show them something in a picture in a book back in school."*

But the farm is more than a classroom for school kids. Volunteers are working to transform the house into a museum.

Jim: *"It really represents ten generations of a family that represent everything in American life."*

They are trying to preserve a past that seems so present on this site, where David Dudley's clothes are still hanging on pegs in the kitchen where he left them the last time he took them off.

Jim: *"This is hands-on history. There's no other place like it locally. The kids can come here and experience all different aspects of the past."*

Hands-on history—at the Dudley Farm, it's positively Connecticut. ■

Melissa Jones School
181 Ledge Hill Rd,
Guilford, CT 06437
3/6/98

Dear Mr. Powers,
    Thank you for coming to Dudley farm. I enjoyed the feild trip. Now I know more about sugaring. I didn't like the maple syrup that much. For breakfast I had waffles with maple syrup on it. It was good. I also liked the black and white kitten.

Sincerely,
Christy Ferris

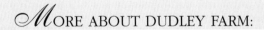

ℳ𝑜𝑟𝑒 ABOUT DUDLEY FARM:

The Dudley Farm hosted more than 4,000 students in 1999. School districts from as far away as New London and Hartford have sent kids to experience seasonal programs such as making maple syrup or rag rugs. Schools can choose from twenty-five activities or lessons. The Dudley Farm is open to the public from 10:00 A.M. to 1:00 P.M. on weekdays and from 10:00 A.M. to 2:00 P.M. on Saturdays. For information call (203) 457-0770. ■

FOR HONOR AND VALOR

Veterans Day must be bittersweet for John Motley, a Vietnam vet. The day is meant to honor all men and women who have served their country, but the service of African-American veterans has often been overlooked.

John Motley is frequently asked to speak to community groups about the service of African-Americans in the Armed Forces. It is

a subject he knows well and speaks about passionately.

John: *"My hope is that the message people take away is that blacks have been a part of defending the country from the beginning."*

And John Motley has powerful evidence of the military service blacks have given: His remarkable collection of memorabilia goes all the way back to the American Revolution.

John: *"I do it not to glorify war, but to glorify the role that blacks have played in building this nation."*

Like the black sailors that fought in the war of 1812.

John: *"Here we see a picture of Commodore Oliver Perry's victory at Lake Erie. Blacks were approximately 20 percent of his crew."*

The 1989 Denzel Washington film *Glory* told of the heroism of black troops in the Civil War.

John: *"About 1 percent of the total of the blacks who served in the Civil War were from Connecticut. There were two all-black regiments formed in the state, the 29th Connecticut and the 30th."*

Native Americans dubbed them the "buffalo soldiers."

John: *"In addition to fighting against the Native Americans, they escorted stagecoaches, served as military policemen, and helped to protect the railroads."*

Three hundred fifty thousand blacks served in World War I.

John: *"Half were sent by General Pershing to serve with the French, and they served honorably and were rewarded with the highest military honors."*

John sees irony in World War II, when the Allies fought to topple Hitler and his regime of hate and prejudice, while African-Americans served in segregated military units. Still, men like Dorrie Miller, a hero at Pearl Harbor, and the legendary Tuskegee airmen, made their mark. Black troops proved their bravery again after the Battle of the Bulge.

John: *"When the white forces were decimated and Eisenhower asked for volunteers, thousands of blacks came forward. Even some sergeants volunteered to become privates again to serve."*

Truman ordered the desegregation of the armed forces in 1948, but John Motley says he experienced racism years later while serving as an officer in Vietnam. Still, he is proud of his service, and of his country.

Motley's collection includes over 3,000 items, everything from medals to books, pamphlets, newspaper clippings, and artwork. And there are many personal items, such as discharge papers, which are important documents for historians. If you come across them while cleaning out your attic, he says, don't throw them away. Those documents are a part of the history of defending America that is positively Connecticut. ▨

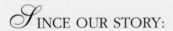

ℐINCE OUR STORY:

John Motley is still adding to his collection. A recent prized find: the documents belonging to Allen Allensworth, the highest-ranking black officer of the late 1800s. President Theodore Roosevelt and his secretary of war William Howard Taft signed the document appointing Allensworth a lieutenant colonel in the Army. Taft, who later became president, is a distant relative of John's wife. John is loaning more than one hundred pieces of his collection to The Charles H. Wright Museum of African American History in Detroit for a yearlong exhibit called "For Honor and Valor." He is also writing a book on the military service of African-Americans and is frequently called on to make presentations in area schools and museums. His main impetus for collecting, he says, is to educate. To contact John for a presentation, e-mail him at: johnmotley@aol.com. ▨

ERA OF IRON

A pleasant walk in the Litchfield Hills is something many of us enjoy, but the lush scenery of today would have been unrecognizable to the people who lived and worked there from 1730 to 1923, when more than two dozen blast furnaces operated along the Blackberry River. The remains of several survive.

Picturesque village greens, carefully tended homes, and fields framed by rolling wooded hills are all part of the serenity of northwest Connecticut's Litchfield County, where wildflowers flank country streams, winding rivers tumble over waterfalls, and children scramble to net sunnies and crayfish in the shallow waters of the Blackberry River in East Canaan. A time traveler would not recognize the place today, according to Ron Jones. Ron is a member of the committee of volunteers working with industrial historian Ed Kirby of Sharon to preserve a legacy from the age they call the era of iron.

Ron: *"A hundred years ago they would not have seen trees on Canaan Mountain or indeed in many other places. The trees were cut down for charcoal."*

That charcoal was needed to fuel blast furnaces that turned local ore into iron.

Beside a quiet country lane stands a hulking column of Stockbridge marble. This is what's left of one of the last blast furnaces to send plumes of smoke into the sky. The Beckley furnace is named for John Adam Beckley, the man who built it on the banks of the river.

Ron: *"There were more than forty furnaces in the whole area. Streams were*

polluted from things thrown into the water, and there was air pollution and noise pollution from the steady thwamp of the blast from these furnaces."

Ed: *"The iron industry was a major factor in this area for almost 200 years. It began in 1731 with the discovery of iron ore in Salisbury, and they made utensils and things around here until 1925."*

In Ed Kirby's book *Echoes of Iron*, the retired school principal calls the area the "arsenal of the American Revolution."

Ed: *"Over in Salisbury at the furnace built by Ethan Allen, the Forbes brothers, and John Hazeltine, they made iron in 1762. Then when the Revolution broke out, they were producers of cannons. And 42 percent of all the cannons made for the Revolution for the*

Colonists were made right there at that one single furnace."

From the mid-1700s through World War I, the Litchfield iron industry turned out everything from weapons to railroad car wheels.

Men like Milo Barnum and Leonard Richardson developed an iron empire in Connecticut's northwest corner. By the late 1800s their foundry at Lime Rock in Salisbury became the biggest producer of railroad car wheels in the world. Just down the road from the furnace is the final resting place of Samuel Forbes, the man who came to be called "the Iron Prince." He must have been quite a man, because the stories about him are legion, including the one that he was so tough, he washed his hands in molten iron.

But the industry would not last. Pennsylvania-made steel was edging out Connecticut-made charcoal iron, and by 1923 the last of the Litchfield blast furnaces closed, ending Connecticut's iron-making era after nearly two centuries.

The ironmasters who labored here and the buildings that surrounded this furnace

are long gone. The Beckley furnace itself barely survived, though in the 1940s it was declared the state's only industrial monument. State funding for the restoration came just in time to rescue this bit of history.

Ninety-two-year-old Fred Hall, Canaan's historian, is one of the last people to have seen the Beckley furnace in operation. In 1915 he visited with his father, a blacksmith.

Fred: *"One Sunday morning he got a call to come over here to the blast furnace. They were having trouble with the crusher. It had developed a crack in it, and they wanted to save that if they could to keep it going."*

Fred vividly recalls the iron men at work.

Fred: *"I went down and watched them tap the furnace. I saw that molten iron coming out of there, and I remember being terrified. I was fairly close to it, and could feel the heat from where I was standing, like a volcano."*

Less than a decade later the blast furnaces were silent. Discoveries of ore in the West, the vast amounts of water needed to make steel, and new cheaper methods of open-pit mining left Litchfield behind, as steel replaced iron. A Connecticut man won the rights to the Bessemer steel process, developed in England, but he took his business to Pennsylvania.

Ron: *"His friends here said, 'You know this is a great economic advantage for Pittsburgh. Why didn't you bring it back to Connecticut?' And his answer was, 'Because I love Connecticut.'"*

The end of the era of iron allowed the industrial scars to heal in East Canaan.

Ron: *"The fascinating thing to me is that, unlike any other project I have ever worked on, we never had any opposition. People would come from all over and say, 'Yes, the furnace should be saved.' It is a symbol of this old heritage that we have, and it is a special symbol because it reminds us of when this was an industrial area and not the beautiful Litchfield Hills it is today."*

So these volunteers saved the Beckley furnace as a symbol of a time gone by that was positively Connecticut. ■

*M*ORE:

The state is acquiring the house beside the Beckley furnace, which was once the paymaster's office, and some land nearby for further historic site development. Eventually Beckley will be the focal point of seven sites on an Iron Heritage Trail. For more information, contact the Litchfield Hills Travel Council at (860) 567–4506. ■

Animals and
Their People

BACK ON THE FARM

Although increasing development and economics have convinced some farmers in Connecticut to sell their land, one family has reversed the trend of giving up family farms by resurrecting one that had not been farmed in forty years.

On an April afternoon when the temperature is tickling the eighty-degree mark, these bouncing babies have a bad case of spring fever. This season's crop of lambs at Sankow's Beaver Brook Farm in Lyme are out for a frolic while their moms nibble the tender shoots of grass just popping up in the pasture.

Suzanne Sankow started raising sheep after raising her six kids.

Suzanne: *"We started with five or six sheep, and that was acceptable for a suburban family."*

Now there are more than 600 East Frislands, Romneys, and natural coloreds. What began as a hobby became a way to hold onto the land her husband's grand-

father, Buzzell Sankow, bought in 1917 for $2,000. The land hadn't been farmed for decades.

Suzanne: *"I'm doing it to have income to pay the expenses of the farm and to be able to have one of our children take this over."*

Suzanne and her husband, Stan, gave up the country-club life and a house on Block Island to reestablish this farm. It's clear Suzanne loves every part of the operation, whether she's wandering through the barn . . .

Suzanne: *"I usually do the evening lamb check at two in the morning, for baby lambs. I like being in the barn alone and I like being with the animals. I never need to use an alarm clock."*

. . . or stroking the fine fleece she sells washed and carded or raw, right off the

sheep's back. That fleece is not dyed or chemically treated, just gently washed before it is spun into yarn, also for sale at the farm. Some of the yarn goes into the sweaters, hats, mittens, and boiled wool vests she sells in the wool shop. Some goes into making her wonderfully warm Connecticut blankets.

In the butcher shop Stan is trimming a leg of lamb. The Sankows sell their own meat, free of antibiotics and without added hormones.

Inside the barn, the sheep are lining up for milking. Suzanne's son-in-law Bryan Farnham is helping out.

Bryan: *"Sheep don't milk like cows do, for as long a period. They usually give milk for only three to four months."*

And while the sheep are producing milk, Suzanne is turning out yogurt and cheese. The feta and summer savory are fresh cheeses; the farmstead and Pleasant Valley are aged hard cheeses. She calls sheep cheese "the gourmet cheese of the world."

Direct sales of their meat, cheese, and wool have made it possible for the Sankows to restore their family's farming tradition.

Suzanne: *"There is nothing else that I'd rather do. I'm very lucky to find what I enjoy."*

Enjoying a way of life, rooted in the past, that is positively Connecticut. ∎

𝒫.𝒮.:

I love to visit the farm in the spring, when the lambs are gamboling through the pastures, but a visit anytime is a great experience. On the Saturday after Thanksgiving the Sankows hold an open house that combines a farm tour with horse-drawn wagon rides and demonstrations of shearing and spinning. Sankow's Beaver Brook Farm is located at 139 Beaver Brook Road in Lyme and is open year round, seven days a week, from 9:00 A.M. to 9:00 P.M. Call (860) 434–2843. ∎

SIGNS OF LOVE

A Killingworth woman is so devoted to her dogs that she calls her home *Three Dogs Inn* in their honor, takes them away to summer camp for canines, and saved their lives when other families had turned their backs on them.

Dalmatians Hogan and Georgia inhabit a world of silence, a world in which they cannot hear the bark of another dog or the call of their owner, Connie Bombaci. Connie believes as many as one in ten dalmatians is deaf, the result of their tremendous popularity, which led to inbreeding. Often deafness leads to a sorry fate.

Connie: *"Many of the deaf dogs, once they're discovered to be deaf by the breeder or their new home, are put down."*

Some owners don't realize their dogs are deaf. Connie recently observed a family having some trouble walking a dog on a leash.

Connie: *"I said, 'Is your dog deaf?' And they said, 'Oh no, he just doesn't like to listen to us.'"*

When an owner thinks a dog is deliberately disobeying, it can lead to frustration and sometimes to abuse or abandonment. That's how Connie and Jim Bombaci came to adopt their first dalmatian.

Connie: *"He had been abused. He was thin and skittish. We had to build up his self-confidence. He wasn't even housebroken at eighteen months old."*

Friends tried to talk her out of adopting a deaf dog, but the veteran teacher was undaunted.

Connie: *"I guess being a teacher you just learn to take care of different needs."*

Connie and Jim, who already had a black Lab named India, brought the dalmatian home and named him Hogan.

Connie: *"'Hogan' is a Native American word for shelter or home, and we promised him that he would never be without a home again."*

Connie couldn't speak to Hogan as she could to her hearing dog, India. But she figured if humans could learn sign language, so could dogs. First she taught herself, and then she taught him.

Connie: *"The first word that I usually teach is 'cookie,' because once the dog understands and gets a cookie, they're watching my hands all the time hoping for a cookie."*

Soon Connie and Jim brought home another needy pooch, named Georgia. After months of training, Hogan and Georgia understand more than forty signs and entire sentences. Connie has other ways to communicate with the dogs, like catching their attention with a flashlight when it's too dark to see her hands.

Connie is spreading the message about training deaf dogs through the Internet. She has answered thousands of e-mails from all over, offering advice and training tips.

She shows me how to sign "kiss," and Georgia responds with a big lick. Her system works, resulting in pets that are happy, affectionate, and positively Connecticut. ■

Connie has been promoted to associate principal of Haddam-Killingworth High School. Although her new job keeps her busy, she is still training Hogan, Georgia, and India, who now know more than sixty signs each and have all been certified as therapy dogs. Each Sunday morning they visit a local nursing home with Connie, calling on patients, spending time in their rooms, and bringing their warmth and joy to the place. Owners of deaf dogs can contact Connie through her Web site: www.deafdogs.com. ■

THE SUPREMES

Connecticut is horse country, and Ann Cummings, whose horses have cracked up some pretty big honors, is one of my favorite horse people.

"Supreme" is a good word to describe this flashy pinto stallion, Lee's Apache Kiowa. Just look at him and you get some idea of why he is only the twentieth horse out of some 200,000 American pintos to be named Supreme Champion by the National Pinto Horse Association. The association is dedicated to these showy looking horses, whose distinguishing coats are liberally splashed with white. Kiowa is the pride of the Cummings family and their Five C's Farm in East Lyme.

Ann Cummings: *"Kiowa just wanted to do everything. Nothing ever seemed to make him afraid. He always tried! He might not always understand or do exactly what you wanted, but he was always trying."*

Trained by Michael Cummings (no relation), Kiowa can be ridden either English or

Western style. The stallion has won jumping competitions and is a champion driving horse. He's so good even a novice like me can hop into his carriage and take him for a spin.

Tom Cummings, Ann's husband, says he's rarely seen a horse so versatile.

Tom: *"I think it's brains, his think power."*

The Cummings's love of pintos started when their children were young.

Ann: *"We wanted to surprise our son Thomas for Christmas. It was a really cold dreary day, and we went to see this horse, Patches. She was just ribs and bones and had ice hanging off her. She was in very poor condition, and she was pregnant. We decided to take her home."*

Tom: *"The vet didn't think she would make it, and he said there was no chance that the foal would live."*

Young Thomas nursed Patches back to health. The mare not only survived, she thrived and her baby did, too. The colt became a champion, known as Apache Magic. Patches later gave birth to Kiowa, the Supreme Champion.

Tom Junior was good for Patches, but she turned out to be pretty good for him, too.

Tom Junior: *"Some kids get into trouble, drugs and things, but the horses kept us busy all the time. We never had the chance to go out and experiment with those things."*

All three Cummings kids became national champs, and the next generation of Cummings is already showing promise. Ann and Tom's grandson Alan James Thibodeau isn't even walking yet, but he's already on horseback. The next generation of horses being born here is showing a lot of promise, too. Some are the offspring of Kiowa.

The next great hope for the Cummings's Five C's Farm is a two-year-old colt that may one day be almost as famous as his namesake. He's called Kenny Rogers, after one of Ann and Tom's favorite performers. His daddy was named Gambling Man, and the Cummings are betting on Kenny Rogers to be the next Supreme Champion—something that would be positively Connecticut. ▪

*M*ORE:

Sure enough, Kenny Rogers the colt went on to become a Supreme Champion, too. The Stone Horses Company, which makes models for collectors, has sculpted him as a model horse. Ann and Tom have met Kenny Rogers the singer and become friendly with him. They presented Kenny with photos of his namesake and his Supreme Champion trophy. Kenny writes to them at least once a year, and Ann has even performed with Rogers at one of his concerts, where they sang an impromptu duet of a Christmas carol. ▪

RACING FOR LIFE

Bethany

*G*reyhounds, one of the oldest breeds of dog, appear in art and literature throughout history. Today they are seen mainly at racetracks. But what happens when their racing careers are over? One Connecticut woman wanted to make sure their futures were bright.

Greyhounds. Long ago the Persians believed they carried information into the next world. In ancient Egypt they were mummified and buried along with their royal owners, whose tombs were often deco-

rated with figures of the sleek canines. Alexander the Great is said to have owned one, and General George Custer owned several. Thought to be the fastest of all the breeds, greyhounds were raced 1,000 years before the dawn of horse racing.

Today dog racing is a popular spectator sport, here and in some parts of Europe. In Connecticut the dogs run at the Plainfield Greyhound Park. The average greyhound's career lasts about three years, and when Eileen McCaughern found out that as many as 20,000 were being destroyed when they retired, she took immediate action. She went to the track and persuaded a kennel worker to let her take one of the dogs home.

Eileen: *"Her racing name was Terry Canary, and she was one of fourteen dogs scheduled to be put down that day. They made me promise that if there were any problems, I would bring her back. But she was wonderful, and I fell in love."*

That was twenty-five years ago. Not long after adopting Terry, Eileen formed a rescue group, Retired Greyhounds as Pets, known as REGAP. The group has placed more than 4,000 dogs with families all over Connecticut.

Eileen: *"At first people had a lot of reservations. People have been under the impression*

that greyhounds are very high-strung and vicious because they see the track billboards with the racing muzzles on the dogs. That's totally untrue. They are very mellow and laid-back dogs."

That's how Carol Villardi found them too, except when she and her son Alex take Morgan (formerly known at the track as DD's Martial Law) and Fay (previously known as Fast Phase), out for a little air. Then the dogs pour it on, showing breathtaking speed, racing with each other at speeds up to thirty-five miles an hour without any urging or encouragement. Carol and Alex think their dogs make fine pets, though they did need a little help at first. Racing dogs often have spent most of their lives in kennels and crates, and many have never walked up or down stairs, played with a toy, or ridden in a car.

Carol: *"They are very affectionate and they like all people. That's their criterion: If you're a human being, they love you."*

REGAP operates a retirement farm where the dogs stay until permanent homes are found. All their funding comes from contributions and the fees they charge for adoption.

Eileen: *"I wish we could get some subsidy from the racing industry. I just feel that anyone who makes money from the dogs during their*

racing career should contribute toward their welfare when their track days have ended."

REGAP makes certain demands on the families who take the dogs home. The dogs must be spayed or neutered to prevent breeding, since so many are already produced for the track and so many still need a place to go after the race is over.

Eileen: *"I would love to say one day that we are saving them all, and I will not be happy until that day is here to stay."*

If you care enough to help a greyhound beat the odds, take one home to become part of your family. A retired greyhound could be a pet that's positively Connecticut. ■

SINCE OUR STORY:

The greyhound rescue movement has taken off, and today there are dozens of rescue groups across the country. The Plainfield Greyhound Park now offers its own adoption program.

Eileen McCaughern still runs REGAP of Connecticut. She and her volunteers are often seen at pet supply stores and local home shows, introducing the dogs to the public. If you'd like to help or want to adopt a greyhound, call Eileen at (203) 393–1673 or write to REGAP, P.O. Box 76, Bethany, CT 06524. ■

HIGH HOPES

Old Lyme

*" **H** igh Hopes Therapeutic Riding Inc. was founded in 1974 by some dedicated horsewomen who believed that horses—knowing them, riding them, and caring for them—could make a difference in the lives of people with special needs."—From a High Hopes brochure soliciting volunteers*

There's something about the outside of a horse that's good for the inside of a man. Ronald Reagan used to say that, and Joe Gennaro lives it.

Joe: *"I was a little nervous at first, especially when I first sat up on a horse. But once I was up there and felt my balance, it was a feeling like I haven't felt since I have been in the chair."*

The chair is the wheelchair Joe has used for ten years since a car fell off a mechanic's lift and crushed his spine, leaving him paralyzed.

Diane (walking alongside Joe as he rides): *"Can you describe the feeling you get from riding?"*

Joe: *"I felt tall—very, very tall. I haven't felt that way since the accident."*

For Joe and the other disabled riders, riding is more than fun, it's a form of physical therapy called "hippotherapy." Therapist Carolyn Jagielski explains as she leads a child on horseback around the large indoor equitation ring.

Carolyn: *"The horse's gait mimics our gait. When the rider is seated on the horse's back, the horse's hindquarters move the rider's trunk, in the same way that it would be moving if he were walking."*

That sensation of normal movement helps relax the muscles in the

trunk, increase strength, relieve pain, and improve posture and balance. For a child with cerebral palsy, it also helps improve arm and head control.

All twenty-one horses in the program have been donated to High Hopes. Some have come from the showring, some from a horse lover's backyard. Every one of them has to meet strict criteria. They must be gentle, but not shy. Gait is important. Some are smooth for the most disabled riders; but others have a bumpier motion, which provides more muscle stimulation for riders who can handle it.

Kitty Stalsburg is the program director. She talks as she strokes the neck of Cody, who is sticking his head out over the half-door of his stall.

Kitty: *"This is a people horse. This is a horse that just loves to be with people and that's probably the utmost criteria."*

Cody and the other horses seem almost to understand the role they play in these riders' lives. They help some overcome fear and build self-esteem; others regain their freedom.

As the horses amble along wooded trails, riders can focus on something other than just getting there, because they have someone else's legs to carry them along, Kitty says.

Joe: *"It's really, really nice to be able to walk around and move around without needing a chair or needing braces or anything like that."*

High Hopes, matching people and horses in a way that's positively Connecticut. ■

*M*ORE:

At its Sis Gould Center for Therapeutic Riding, High Hopes works with about 200 riders every week, ranging in age from three to seventy. High Hopes also offers instructor training courses in therapeutic riding to students who come from as far away as Japan and Croatia. Teikyo Post University in Waterbury, working in conjunction with High Hopes, will soon become the first college in the Northeast to offer instructor certification in therapeutic riding as part of its equine management degree. ■

A COASTAL SANCTUARY

T*he Connecticut landscape is dotted with centers for the study of nature and wildlife. One of my favorites is in one of the prettiest spots in all of the state.*

Milford Point, a picturesque spit of land that straddles the Housatonic River and Long Island Sound, was once a get-away for wealthy New Yorkers. Barbara Milton told me a bit about its history.

Barbara: *"In 1868 a man named Smith built a hotel. At that time there was no salt marsh here. This was a large shallow bay full of shellfish. It had been used by the Indians for 10,000 years as a summering ground."*

Today the bay is gone, replaced by the 840-acre Wheeler salt marsh. The hotel is gone too, replaced by a replica that houses the Connecticut Audubon Coastal Center. Among the birds feeding within view are two pairs of osprey returning from their winter migrations. They are nesting on platforms erected in the marsh. Center director Barbara Milton says this salt marsh is much more than a dining room for birds.

Barbara: *"The wetlands act as a filter of pollutants, and they act as a holder of pollutants. They also act as a nursery for not only plankton but for fish and migrating birds. And they provide flood control."*

The center is situated at the mouth of the Housatonic River, and educators here want visitors to know that every drop of water that flows through the watershed eventually flows here, carrying pollution from homes and farms and factories along with it.

Although the name Audubon is synonymous with birds, the coastal center concentrates on what's in Long Island Sound, as well as what flies over it.

Matt Black, the resident naturalist, supervises young visitors as they investigate the touch tank, a 300-gallon saltwater aquarium inhabited by crabs, fish, even shrimp. Under Matt's direction, a group of children eagerly dip their hands in the touch tank's water.

Matt: *"It doesn't look at first glance like you have much in here, but you probably have 500 different animals in here if you look hard enough."*

Matt leads visitors on guided tours of the barrier beach, pointing out the wildlife refuge right next to the center, an area that protects animals from the encroachment of people and development.

If you'd like to learn more about the birds and creatures of Long Island Sound, the center has plenty of special programs, from twice-a-month bird walks, to birthday parties for kids, to family canoe trips.

The new Connecticut Audubon Coastal Center is an educational resource with a mission to preserve the natural resources that are positively Connecticut. ■

ℳORE ON THIS STORY:

The center is now in the midst of the Milford Point Ecosystem Project. More than thirty scientists from the federal and state governments and from several Connecticut colleges, assisted by volunteers, are conducting studies of threatened species, such as the piping plover and the least tern. The outcome of their studies will help conserve and preserve natural habitat in Connecticut. ■

PARTNERS FOR LIFE

New Haven & Bloomfield

W*hen the world grew dark for a New Haven woman, she found a partner—a seeing eye dog—eager and able to help. But it turned out that behind her new canine friend there was an extended family of people who cared, and they really made the difference.*

Lee McGee, an Episcopal priest, is losing her eyesight.

Lee: *"Periodically I will have sudden losses in my vision, and it's very shattering. It means that things that you have been able to do suddenly are obliterated, they're gone."*

As she struggled to cope, Lee turned to prayer.

Lee: *"I regularly fuss with God, and I said, 'You've gotten me to this point. You're going to find a way to help me.'"*

Help came, in the form of a German shepherd, Alex, but not until Lee had suffered a painful lesson.

Lee: *"I had a very serious fall and spent nine months in a cast. I simply misjudged the bottom of a set of stairs. And a friend who had known me twenty years sat me down and said, 'Now look, you need to seriously consider a guide dog.'"*

Twenty-five years ago, when Lee became one of the first women ever ordained an Episcopal priest, macular degeneration had already started to steal her eyesight, yet Lee resisted getting a guide dog.

Lee: *"It meant accepting the growing limitation, and I am a fighter."*

Lee could not imagine a dog in her busy life—teaching at Yale Divinity School, traveling across the country to lead conferences, and preaching in churches like St. Paul and St. James in New Haven, where she was rector.

After her accident, Lee turned to the Fidelco Guide Dog Foundation in Bloomfield. Fidelco has been part of the life's work of a man who is in many ways larger than life. Even at age eighty, at six-foot-five, Charles Kaman is physically imposing, and his accomplishments stand even taller. He invented an innovative guitar, built a billion-dollar aerospace company, and has done so much for the development of helicopter flight that he has won every major award in the field. President Clinton honored him with the National Medal of Technology. Still, he calls the medals and ribbons "junk" and says what counts is helping people. Puppies are his passion, and they are one way that Charlie and his wife, Robbie, have made a difference for many people.

In the 1960s the Kamans started breeding designer German shepherds, dogs that combined heart and character, an instinct to serve, and an intelligence Kaman describes as an astronaut mentality.

Charlie: *"When the blind minister and the dog come to the street corner and she says, 'Forward!', the dog has to make a judgment about whether it's safe. The dog may have to say, 'No, we don't go.' That's disobedience but intelligent disobedience."*

Robbie directs the breeding program that has produced nearly 2,900 puppies since 1960.

Diane: *"When you're breeding these dogs, what's most important? Temperament?"*

Robbie: *"Everything is important. They need to be the right size, can't be too big. They need good health because it's difficult for a dog that doesn't feel well to get up and go to work every day."*

Robbie is at work every day in the kennels, seven days a week, because she has seen these dogs change their partners' lives.

Robbie: *"It isn't that I have to do it. It's something that I choose to do. It's unique to see some of these lives develop and know that you've participated in a part of it. A lot of lasting friendships have been made over the years. It's our extended family."*

Zoë and Tom Tarrant are part of the extended family. The Westport couple and their golden retriever Cody are the foster family raising Izzy, a four-month-old Fidelco pup. Tom's mother needed a guide dog after she lost her sight to retinitis pigmentosa, a condition Tom inherited. One day Tom may need a guide dog.

When Izzy is a little over a year old, the Tarrants will give her back to Fidelco to undergo intensive training that takes a year and costs the nonprofit agency more than $20,000 per dog. The charge to clients is only $150.

Ten years ago Mark Tyler gave up an engineering career to become a trainer for Fidelco.

Mark: "My father worked for a large company for over thirty years. At no time when I was growing up do I remember him coming home and saying that he had an opportunity today to do something significant for somebody else. Fidelco gives us the

opportunity, me especially as an employee, to know that what I did each day with the dogs, and with the people, probably had a significant impact on somebody's life."

The last stage of each guide dog's training takes place on their new partner's home turf, a concept Fidelco pioneered, and one that fine-tunes a dog to handle its new responsibilities. For Lee McGee's dog Alex, that means traveling by airplane and train (he even gets her suitcases off the luggage carousel) and handling the university environment of Yale with its busy New Haven streets, as well as the quiet of a church sanctuary. But Lee says thanks to Alex, she does God's work better.

Lee: "I've learned a lot about God from Alex. I know that sounds trite, but I can't tell you what it means to have this animal committed to my safety and well-being, day in and day out, minute by minute, hour by hour. These dogs want to protect so much that they would give their lives! That kind of single-hearted devotion to me as a person is something that I've never experienced, even with the love of my family. And it suddenly dawned on me a year or two into it, this must be what the love of God is like."

Alex and Lee—thanks to Fidelco, they are partners for life who are positively Connecticut. ■

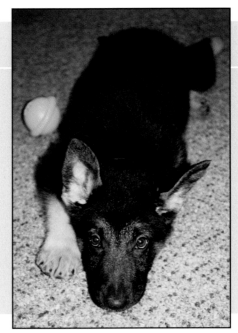

*M*ORE:

Want to "share the vision"? Join Fidelco's fundraising Walk-Run-Ride held each May at their campus in Bloomfield. Make a donation, or be a foster family for a Fidelco puppy. For more information write Fidelco Guide Dog Foundation, P.O. Box 142, Bloomfield, CT 06002, call (860) 243-5200, or visit the Web site www.fidelco.org. ■

Helping Hands

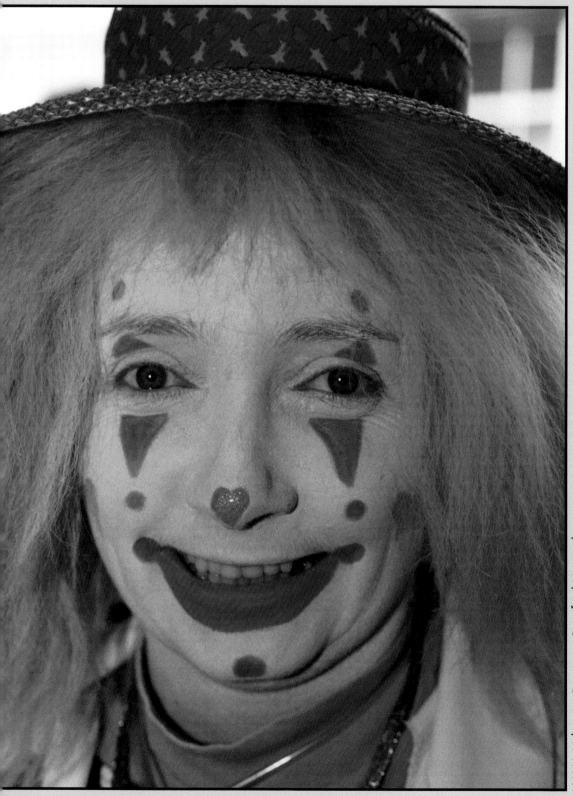

HAHA Volunteer Program, Stamford Hospital

A GIFT BY THE SEA

Waterford

There's a little bit of Newport on the Connecticut shoreline in Waterford. And this mansion belongs to you. It's called Eolia, after the island home of Aeolus, the Greek god of winds, and when a sea breeze sweeps off Long Island Sound and across the great expanse of lawn, it's easy to see how it got its name.

Eolia was the summer home of Edward and Mary Harkness. In 1924 Edward Harkness was the fourth richest man in the

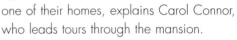

United States. This forty-two-room Italian-style villa was just

one of their homes, explains Carol Connor, who leads tours through the mansion.

Carol: "Edward's father, Stephen, invested $60,000 as a silent partner with John D. Rockefeller, and that was how Standard Oil began. The Harknesses did live very graciously, but they were philanthropic. Most of their money was given to health and education. Two hundred million dollars, as a matter of fact."

An army of eighty servants maintained the mansion, the gardens, and the farm on more than 230 acres fronting Long Island Sound. When Mary Harkness died in

1950, she left the estate to the people of Connecticut, as a park and recreation area. But over the years dwindling budgets left the home in disrepair.

Carol: *"It was collapsing and boarded up. The materials in the pillars, the standards, the cement blocking in the archways—that all had to be replaced."*

In 1992 when the Department of Environmental

Protection's plans for restoration stalled, a group of concerned citizens stepped in, calling themselves the Friends of Harkness. One member, Marcella Wagner, says they lobbied for release of state funds and oversaw the $3.6 million restorations of the mansion and formal gardens.

Marcella: *"The Friends of Harkness sent away for the*

blueprints by renowned garden designer Beatrix Farrand, which had been donated to a college in California. Every weekend, for many many weeks, a group of forty or fifty volunteers replanted this garden bulb for bulb, plant for plant."

Today families stroll the parklike grounds, the beach, the gardens, even the elegant pergola where Mary Harkness used to sip her afternoon tea. The mansion can be rented for weddings and parties.

Marcella thinks the Harknesses would be pleased if they could see their former home today.

Marcella: *"They shared their money, their time, and their encouragement with other people. Hopefully that's what Harkness Park is all about."*

Harkness Park, a special place for people that's positively Connecticut. ■

*M*ORE:

Every bride longs to feel like a princess on her wedding day, and at Harkness you will. A bridal couple has the complete run of the mansion the day of the wedding, and in good weather the ceremony can be held outdoors in the amphitheater. Rental is $3,500 for five hours and includes use of a tent, dance floor, tables, and chairs. Eolia is available for rental March 1 through December 23. For details on park hours and mansion rental, call (860) 443–5725. ■

SAVING THE YALE HOUSE

Wallingford

Many historic homes are disappearing, but in one town some folks have gone to great trouble to preserve a piece of the past.

The heart of Wallingford is in its heritage; that's what the keepers of its history believe. So when The Home Depot planned to build a store on North Colony Road, and a 210-year-old house was in the way, the town's Historic Preservation Trust took action.

Jerry Farrell is a town councilor and the trust president.

Jerry: *"We have maybe a dozen and a half buildings in town dating from the eighteenth century. Each and every one of them would be hard to lose. We lose touch with that period of time every time we lose one of these buildings."*

But was the home known as the Yale House worth saving? John LeTourneau, a member of the trust, wasn't sure until he took a close look.

John: *"We started going with the pluses and minuses of the old house. When all was said and done, there were more pluses than minuses."*

It took nearly three years to work out the details of how to go about saving the house that stood near the Yankee Silversmith restaurant. Simply moving it was not an option, because of the nearby parkway and a railroad overpass. The solution: Dismantle the house, store it, and eventually erect it on another site. The owner donated the house, and The Home Depot agreed to delay construction so it could be taken apart piece by piece.

Preservationist Jeffrey Bradley of Westbrook was reluctant to take on the project. For one thing, he suspected the home had been remodeled (he calls it "remuddled") so many times that there might not be enough original architecture worth saving. But eventually Jeff signed on for the project.

Jeff: *"The more time I spent with the house, the more trips I made, I began to slowly grow fond of it."*

More than once, John LeTourneau wondered if they'd made a mistake.

John: *"There was a new fireplace, new wall paneling. New, new, new, everything was new. It was very discouraging."*

But as Jeff and John took crowbars to some of the walls, they began to uncover what Jeff calls the secrets of the Yale House. A significant amount of original detail had survived.

Jeff: *"In most remodeling today, a room is gutted and thrown in a Dumpster and it's gone forever. In this case most of the fabric was here and hidden behind walls."*

Colonial-era crown moldings were discovered beneath false ceilings. Original fireplaces and beehive ovens were uncovered behind Victorian mantelpieces. In the sitting room a little detective work revealed evidence of a missing corner cupboard, which may have been sold to an antiques collector.

Jeff: *"All the original nail lines and the handsplit lath prove that the original cupboard was there. We have found someone who has information about its possible whereabouts. It would be nice to get it back."*

Not much is known about the original owners, but they might have been related to the founder of Yale University. Their fine home stood the test of time, two centuries of it.

Jeff: *"This was no farmer foraging a house out of the woods. This is truly someone who had the resources to have a great house built."*

In an upstairs chamber the plaster walls are peeled off, revealing original handsplit lath and thousands of rose-head nails.

Jeff: *"There was a blacksmith working for months, literally months, just making nails for the house."*

At 6 foot 6, Jeff doesn't need a ladder for the overhead work. He reaches up and wriggles an oak ceiling joist out of the place it has rested in for more than 200 years, saying, *"This is how you take a house apart."*

Jeff: *"This house was nothing more than a kit in the eighteenth century. It was fabricated on the ground. Each one of these beams or joists has the Roman numerals on it."*

This method of construction made it easier to put the house up in traditional barn-raising style, with neighbors and friends coming from all over to help.

Someday, when the trust can afford to put the house up again, John LeTourneau hopes to organize a twenty-first-century barn raising to teach today's builders, contractors, and homeowners the craft of the eighteenth century.

John: *"Then they could go into their communities and perhaps save a building. We get calls constantly—'Can you show us how to do plaster work?' or 'We've just bought an old house and we don't know what to do and we're afraid that we're going to do it wrong.'"*

To make sure they do it right, Jeff has painstakingly documented the house with elaborate maps, field notes, blueprints, and photographs. As layer after layer of the house was peeled back, Jeff found more and more artifacts hidden inside. He cataloged each one. They ranged from an 1809 dime, to a bit of mud that was some of the original mortar, to natural insulation used in the attic—the chaff from wheat.

Jeff: *"We're at a critical stage of losing our historic homes and the fabric that the country was built on. There's not many left, and the need for proper information is enormous."*

Jeff and his crew labored nearly seven weeks taking the house apart. On one of the last days, one of the last families to live in the house stopped by to reminisce. Mary Meyer Brooks and her sister Peggy Meyer Gopoian remembered how their parents treasured the house next door to their restaurant.

Mary: *"We wouldn't have this house here for the preservation trust or for anyone to enjoy in the future if it weren't for my parents, Robert and Esther Meyer."*

Peggy: *"To actually see it little by little being taken down, not falling down or pushed down, is just fantastic. I stopped here to kind of say good-bye to it."*

So did a daughter and granddaughter, so three generations of Meyers watch as Jeff packs up the last pieces into three huge trailers.

Diane (to Jeff): *"Do you ever see yourself being put out of business because there are no old houses to be saved anymore, because too many get hit with a wrecking ball and disappear?"*

Jeff: *"Yes, there is definitely an end to it, and the end is in sight. They are as endangered as any whales in the ocean. There are so few left."*

But one more is left . . . one survivor of the eighteenth century that is positively Connecticut. ■

More:

Many antique buildings that are moved are not eligible for the National Historic Register, which can affect funding to preserve them. The Yale House may be eligible, because the trust saved the foundation stone, so that the house can be erected again, in a new place, on its 200-year-old base. ■

SUBMARINE CENTENNIAL

T*he submarine force has always been known as "the silent service," but in the year 2000 they were making a lot of noise, celebrating a one-hundreth anniversary!*

Seaman James Young (Carlsberg, Pennsylvania): *"When I was younger I watched movies like* Hunt for Red October. *I thought it would be cool to be on one."*

Seaman Marcez Jackson (Shreveport, Louisiana): *"I've seen more places and I've experienced so much and have met so many people."*

Seaman Michael Richard Parks (Waterbury, Connecticut): *"You see all the stuff you see in the movies, and its like, hey, that's what I'm doing!"*

Maybe because of the submarine's tradition of silence, our fascination with submarines runs deep. From the earliest attempt, David Bushnell's *Turtle* in 1776, to the first modern-day submarine delivered by John Holland to the U.S. Navy in 1900, to today's nuclear-powered submarine fleet, we have marveled at how men live and wage war beneath the ocean. Since 1916 every submariner has learned those secrets at the Naval Submarine Base New London in Groton.

Inside electronic classrooms, young sailors learn on computers before moving to simulators and then on to submarines.

Petty Officer Second Class Robert Crossno: *"They can minimize their lab time to one-third of what it used to be because they've made the mistakes up here on the computer. Now they can go down to the training units and step through it flawlessly."*

Instructors teach more than 190 courses at sub school, including fire fighting, escape, and damage repair. Thirty thousand students go through the school each year, graduating to subs like the USS *Philadelphia*, a fast-

attack submarine commissioned in 1977. The first of the Los Angeles class, the sub is about the length of a football field and has been retrofitted with a dry-deck shelter to deliver Navy Seals for covert operations or rescue missions. Our tour guide is Kevin Crisman, the Chief of the Boat. His crew calls him "COB."

COB Crisman: *"This is the heart center of the ship, where the officer of the deck stands watch on what we call the conn."*

This is a world without windows, where periscopes peer outside and sonar takes the place of sight.

Petty Officer Brian Locke mans the sonar control room: "We put away our eyes and just steer with what we hear."

The sailors on watch in the control station steer the 7,000-ton sub and maintain the underwater depth ordered by the chief with a precision of plus or minus 6 inches.

COB Crisman: *"This is the first watch they stand. I've got seventeen- and eighteen-year-old kids here driving my multibillion-dollar submarine."*

Crisman slides on his palms down a ladder leading to the torpedo room two decks below the control station, where four 21-inch tubes can launch torpedoes and Tomahawk missiles. The torpedo room also provides a few extra "racks," or sleeping berths, for an overflow crew. In the berthing areas, living quarters for each man amount to a bunk for sleeping and storage that is less than 15 square feet in size. It will provide his only privacy for missions of up to six months long.

Base Commander Captain Ray Lincoln: *"We're brothers because we live in close quarters and we're a small crew. There are no extra people on board a sub. Everybody is essential."*

The line of submariners stretches back to the dawn of the twentieth century, when John Holland sold his first sub to the Navy for $150,000. It was powered by a gas engine for surface running and electric motors for submerged operations. The newly expanded Submarine Force Library and Museum in Groton traces the development of the diesel-powered subs of World War II. After Pearl Harbor devastated the surface fleet, submarines became America's primary offensive weapons in the Pacific Theater, sinking 30 percent of the Japanese Navy and destroying 60 percent of the Japanese merchant force. But the so-called "silent victory" came at a heavy price. Fifty-two subs were lost. A monument in Groton honors the 3,500 submariners who died.

Dick Eng is a retired submarine veteran.

Dick: *"That's one of our goals for the sub vets organization—to perpetuate the memory of these guys who gave their lives."*

During the Cold War submarine warfare changed forever. In 1955 Admiral Hyman Rickover launched the first nuclear-powered submarine—the *Nautilus*, now decommissioned and on display at the museum. Dick Eng sailed on both, the old diesels and the nuclear-powered subs.

Dick: *"It's quite a change, like going from the Pony Express to jet airplanes."*

Lieutenant Commander Ben Howard directs the sub museum. He talked about the "Rickover effect."

Commander Howard: *"By putting nuclear power plants into the subs, we were able to make them truly submersible. They were no longer dependent on the atmosphere at all. We could operate at higher speeds for indefinite periods. And nuclear power allowed us to put subs out to sea with nuclear missiles on board, keep them continuously submerged, and make them impossible to find."*

The end of the Cold War has seen a rise in regional conflicts, and the sub force has responded from Desert Storm to Kosovo.

Captain Lincoln: *"I see the sub as being an extremely flexible and multimission tool for the joint task force commander because of the capability brought to the table in terms of such warfare missions as strike, special force operations, and reconnaissance."*

And as long as there are submarines, Lincoln says that Submarine Base New London will be the submarine capital of the world.

Captain Lincoln: *"I think we have a very deep-rooted sense that this is our home, because our soul is here."*

It's where the U.S. Postal Service honored one hundred years of submarine service with a series of commemorative submarine postage stamps.

At the ceremony Congressman Sam Gejdenson talked about the integral role subs have played in the region.

Congressman Gejdenson: *"When you look at eastern Connecticut, this is the heart of what's built our economy and led to a sense of who we are as a community."*

A community on base and on board that is positively Connecticut. ■

𝓜ORE:

The addition to the Submarine Force Library and Museum located on the Thames River in Groton opened in 2000, as part of the submarine centennial celebration. The expansion adds a new theater, a classroom for visiting school groups, a larger research library, and more archival storage area. The collections include more than 5,000 volumes, 18,000 artifacts, 20,000 documents, and 30,000 photos. The Nautilus, the first nuclear-powered submarine, is a National Landmark and can be boarded by museum visitors. ☐

DOCTORS OF MIRTH

Stamford

Connecticut has a long history with the circus. This is the home of P. T. Barnum, after all. But not all of Connecticut's clowns are found under the big top.

A clown dressed in mechanic's overalls, carrying a large white plastic bone, enters a patient's room at Stamford Hospital. It's Dr. Goodwrench, a.k.a. Emmett Brown.

Dr. Goodwrench: *"Hi! I'm Dr. Goodwrench. I got this funny bone down at the lab, and we're supposed to make a delivery."*

Tickling funny bones is the specialty of Dr. Goodwrench and his partner Dr. Make-a-Wish, also known as Paulette Esposito. She touches the funny bone and bursts out laughing.

Dr. Make-a-Wish: *"Yep, it works all right!"*

They are MDs—doctors of mirth—specially trained to cheer up patients. Brown and Esposito are two of thirty clown volunteers in HAHA—the Health and Humor Associates program. In real life Emmett is a lawyer.

Emmett: *"It keeps me balanced and gives me a little perspective."*

In the lounge one clown is making up another's face. Richard Ward is one of the newest HAHA volunteers. His wife, Mary Lou, has been Dr. Sera Heartburn for three years.

Richard: *"She would come home from the hospital and be full of joy and happiness. After a couple of years, I started to get envious. I asked if I could at least try it, and here I am."*

The clowns are known for their gently silly, sometimes corny routines. Dr. Lotsa Dots (Claudia Boerst) says she's in cardiology, because she does card tricks. The clowns poke fun at everything from hospital red tape to hospital food, but they also know when to listen. When Dr. Lotsa Dots hands patient Vincent Zaccagnino a limp rubber chicken, saying "I got something special for your dinner," the response injects a bit of somber reality.

Vincent: *"Does the chicken have toes? Because I am about to lose some of mine."*

The clowns know when a word of encouragement makes a difference. Sister

Jolancia Koslinski, a Catholic nun, is also a nurse.

Sister Jolancia: *"My brother just had surgery yesterday, and he was so downhearted. I saw the clowns and I said, 'Hey, come in here for a while.' They made my brother laugh, and he forgot about the pain in his leg, at least temporarily. Spread some joy, that's what our world is about."*

Sometimes the staff needs a smile as much as the patients do. Krista Podolski, a nurse, looks forward to the visits.

Krista: *"They really open up our hearts and make us feel a little better so we can pass it along to our patients later that day."*

Penny Smith, a former cancer patient, observed the Big Apple circus clowns visiting sick kids at a New York City hospital and was inspired to start the HAHA program at Stamford Hospital. She saw the joy a clown brings to a

Stamford Hospital trains a new class of clowns every eighteen months. They visit the pediatric floor, nursing home, and hospice. To get involved call Bonnie Jennings Steele, the Director of Volunteer Services at Stamford Hospital, at (203) 325–7521. ◾

child's face and thought anyone stuck in the hospital could use a dose of that. Dawn Palmer, known as Dr. Crockpot, agrees.

Dawn: *"To leave a patient with a smile when they're fretful or anxious to go home—that's what it's all about."*

It's all about clowning and caring in a way that's positively Connecticut. ◼

MORE CLOWNING AROUND
New Haven

Other hospitals are inviting clowns to join their health care teams, too. A foundation begun by the parents of a patient at Yale New Haven Children's Hospital brings the Big Apple Circus Clown Care Unit in to make life a bit more cheerful for kids who are sick. The unit, started by Michael Christensen, cofounder of the Big Apple Circus, consists of professional clowns who spend their time performing chocolate milk transfusions, red nose transplants, and just about anything else they can think of to bring a smile to the face of a child. ◼

SHOW TIME

Hamden, New Haven & Stamford

Each day on Metro-North trains packed with sometimes cranky commuters, conductor Travis Ford spreads a little cheer as he works his way down the aisle. As the 2:30 pulls out of Stamford for Grand Central, it's show time.

Travis: *"Tickets, tickets, tickets! I'll take any kind of ticket, as long as it's not a parking ticket. I'll even take a lotto ticket, but it's got to be a winner!"*

After punching tickets and collecting fares, Travis adds a little something extra, the weather report.

Travis: *"Sunday, variable cloudiness with a mixture of sun and clouds. Monday, cloudy with shower activity. I wish you all a good day today! You owe it to yourself to have a nice evening."*

The passengers applaud, and Travis bows deeply.

Travis: *"It all started when a passenger said, 'I wonder what it's going to be like today?' And I told him 'It's going to be 70 degrees, and the winds are 10 miles an hour,' and I wondered, 'What did I say that for?' Then the passengers started smiling and clapping and, well, it's history now."*

Max Mallol has been riding the trains from Fairfield for a decade. Travis is her favorite forecaster.

Max: *"You watch the people on the TV news and they're always wrong! You never know what to wear. But when you listen to him, you know exactly what to wear."*

And whom to root for.

Travis: *"Have a Yankee type of day, a winning day! I'll be back with some ball scores in a little while."*

Travis even offers stock market updates. The train may be a local, but his commentary is nonstop.

Travis: *"This is it, Grand Central Station, your last, your final stop. Everybody out of the pool!"*

Passenger Carolyn Gregory says mornings aren't the same when Travis's schedule changes.

Carolyn: *"He greets everyone very warm and friendly. Those who came on the* train tired and frowning left totally different!"

Travis: *"I tell them you gotta leave that paranoia outside the door. You can't bring it into the train."*

As passengers stream out of the car, Travis has a good-bye for some, a handshake or hug for others. A few minutes after arriving in Grand Central, it's time to head back to Connecticut, this time on the 4:14 to New Haven. He calls his regular riders the 414 Club.

Travis: *"Members of the 414 Club, please have your tickets ready. Oh, look at that—he was born ready, this guy."*

Some passengers deliberately miss their trains if they know Travis is assigned to the next one.

Travis: *"Sometimes people have down days and I try to pull 'em up, you know. I try to give as much of myself to the person as I can."*

A passenger from Easton has known Travis thirteen years: *"He's got such a positive attitude. He obviously enjoys his job."*

But Travis is considering a job change. He has been featured on TV so many times, he's thinking of a career on the air. Travis says he might give up riding the rails if the right offer came along. And riding the train through Fairfield County you can bet he meets a lot of the right people, including broadcasting executives and high-powered talent agents.

Travis: *"I'd love to do the weather and sports. I've known so many people. Who knows? I might be able to get the ratings up."*

But for now, Travis Ford has his own stage.

Travis: *"I'll say good-bye to you now—auf Wiedersehen, a rivederci, sayonara, ciao, hasta luego and adios, good-bye, so long, and farewell. If I missed anyone, I'm sorry. Shalom. Nostrovya."*

He goes on in Celtic, Danish, Swahili, Chinese, Filipino, and finishes with a flourish.

Travis: *"And of course, if you're French, au revoir. God bless you and have a super good day today!"*

In any language, Travis Ford is spreading a little sunshine that's positively Connecticut. ■

MORE:

Travis Ford is considering retirement soon. He says he's eager to spend more time with his family and pursue that TV career. ■

SOUVENIRS OF CONNECTICUT'S PAST

Fairfield

Most of us have not visited all 169 towns and cities in Connecticut. But one man has not only visited them all, but has also worked in each one: artist Robert Conrad Ledoux.

Outside the Unquowa Hotel in Fairfield, that's where I first met Robert Conrad Ledoux, in 1994. He was sketching the old building, trying to capture its image before time ran out. The previous winter's snow, and rain saturation, had sealed its death warrant. The antique from the 1870s was slated for demolition, but Bob was determined to save her memory.

Bob: *"Photographs and paintings and drawings will be the only thing we leave to the future as to how these things were."*

We met again three years later as Bob was hanging the lithograph he made from that sketch in a one-man show at Gallery 56 in Meriden.

Bob: *"The building has since been demolished. It was in a dilapidated state and had been condemned. And I'd say it's typical of the kind of loss of our historic stock that comes through neglect."*

Saving Connecticut's landmarks, at least on paper, is what Bob's artwork is all about. He's just finished a six-year project to paint or draw at least one image from each of the 169 towns in Connecticut.

Bob: *"I think I burned out like five vehicles in that time. When you're starting and stopping the vehicles a lot, you tend to burn the engines out."*

But it was worth it. He couldn't stop the wrecking balls or the ravages of time, but Bob saved for us some of what Connecticut was, and will never be again. Bob set up his easel near cider mills and water wheels and town greens and village halls. Some of these structures exist now only in history, but Bob's paintings and lithographs bring them back—such as the roller coaster that once dominated the amusement park at Savin Rock. His portfolio of houses is thicker than a real estate agent's, filled with images of the array of historic homes that once stood on every corner.

Bob: *"This is kind of a commentary on our times. Connecticut is changing so rapidly. We're losing an awful lot of it."*

The title of Bob's show at Gallery 56 was "Souvenirs of the 20th Century," appropri-

ate since many of the places he has pictured may not last beyond the end of the century. In fact, about 10 percent of the buildings in these pictures have disappeared since he began the project. Bob estimates that one hundred years from now, only 10 percent will remain.

Bob: *"To me these buildings and communities are very important, and I'm happy when I'm drawing them."*

Working on this project, he made an important discovery about the citizens of Connecticut.

Bob: *"People are very proud of their communities . . . whether it be the largest in the state, Bridgeport or Hartford, or a small rural area."*

Still, landmarks are disappearing.

Bob: *"Sometimes from inaction, action takes place—and that's the problem with our historic buildings, because each one of them needs care and attention in the local communities."*

That's the message in the work of Robert Conrad Ledoux, an artist who is positively Connecticut. ■

$\mathcal{M}$ORE ABOUT THIS STORY:

Bob is at work on a new series of paintings and lithographs of Atlantic Coast lighthouses from Maine to Texas. He estimates there are eight hundred of them, and so far he has visited about three hundred and painted one third of those. He's even re-creating light-houses of the past that have been demolished by the sea, storms, or man. When not in the field, or plying the Atlantic in his 8-foot inflatable Zodiac, Bob works from his studio in Fairfield.

Most weekends find him selling his paintings and lithographs at art shows. To find out where he'll be next, check out his Web site: http://hometown.aol.com/ligthouse1. □

TEAM GILLETTE

East Haddam

The actor William Gillette must have loved autumn at his hilltop home, with its commanding views of brilliant foliage. In 1944 the place that's come to be known as Gillette Castle became a state park. Some people with a passion for the park are dedicated to making it a better place.

A noted actor from the turn of the century through the mid-1920s, William Gillette was especially famous for his portrayal of Sherlock Holmes. Now Gillette's East Haddam estate, one of  Connecticut's most beloved landmarks, is in the middle of a major renovation. Park superintendent Donald Goss says the first step is making the house watertight.

Don: *"Water comes in through the stone in the wintertime. It freezes and thaws and separates the stone."*

Stonemasons are replacing parapet walls, adding flashing, restoring balconies, and re-creating a dragon-head gargoyle on Gillette's fanciful twenty-four-room castle.

Don: *"Basically they have to dig out all the old mortar, throw away their levels and their squares, and be a little artistic—refit the stones in there and let them stick out all sorts of ways and make it look ragged."*

Or rustic, as Gillette might have described it.

Though the castle is closed during the renovation, the spectacular grounds are open, thanks in part to a dedicated group of workers who call themselves Team Gillette. Don Goss directs their work.

Don: *"Well, ladies and gentlemen, today we are going to work on the trail, and we're going to install water bars, and we're going to do the stone edging and bring in fill."*

One of the volunteers calls out, "What time is lunch?" and the rest laugh, but soon they are hard at work, sometimes side by side with park employees. They clear trails, raking and piling brush, and build new benches for hikers. Ed Wininger is a retired firefighter who often brings his grandkids along.

Diane: *"At the end of the day, when you look at how you spent the day, how do you feel?"*

Ed: *"I feel good, especially since my grandson enjoyed making the benches and other stuff with the hand tools."*

Chuck Oakes heads the Friends of Gillette Castle State Park, the formal name of Team Gillette.

Chuck: *"This is an opportunity for people to really make a difference in their backyard. To come out and do something and find immediate gratification in building a bench or clearing a trail."*

Or pitching in on another project, such as restoring Gillette's beloved railroad, which he called the Seven Sisters Shortline, after the seven hills in the area. Some of that work will take place across the river in Chester at Essex Motor Sports. It's now a motorcycle workshop, where Ted Tine restores classic bikes. It's fitting that photocopies of Gillette's handwritten plans for the train are spread across Ted's desk. Research shows the train was built at this very shop when a Mr. E. N. Priest owned it.

Twenty miles away in Portland, at the central supply depot of the Department of Environmental Protection, the train is stored in a garage, alongside cast-off computers and office furniture. Bob Guyon, another volunteer, peels blankets off the individual cars as he describes the workmanship.

Bob: *"It was designed with all wooden latches. This side opened up to allow two people per seat. Of course the people then were a little smaller than we are today."*

After Gillette's death the train became a popular attraction at Lake Compounce Amusement Park in Bristol, where it went through retrofitting over the years. Bob estimates it will take a team of volunteers over a year to restore the locomotive to its original condition. Someday he hopes to see the train running at the castle again.

Bob: *"We have it, and it would be a shame to lose it. We should pass it on to people in the future so they can see what life was like at one time."*

Gillette Castle isn't the only park to ignite this passion in volunteers. The Friends of Connecticut State Parks is an umbrella organization for a dozen groups of volunteers who do everything from lobbying for funding for state parks, to running gift shops, to weeding gardens. Park officials say the Friends organization played a critical role in supporting the governor's program to spend $114 million to improve the state's parks.

At Gillette Castle, the Friends say their mission is clear, and their role model is the man who built this estate.

Chuck: *"He was a Renaissance personality. This group is basically patterned after him. Our charge is to work with the state as a partner to keep the spirit of Gillette alive."*

In a spirit of volunteerism that is positively Connecticut! ■

Since Our Story:

The $5 million restoration of Gillette Castle took longer than anticipated because the damage was more extensive than initially realized. The castle should reopen in spring 2001. Even with the castle closed, 190,000 people visited the park in 1999. If you'd like to join the Friends of Gillette Castle State Park, call the castle at (860) 526–2336. ■

GUARDING HISTORY

New Haven

April 2000 marked the 225th anniversary of the charter grant to the Second Company Governor's Footguard of Connecticut and the departure of the command in 1775 to Cambridge, Massachusetts, on Powder House Day.

From the time he was a boy and first spotted their foot-tall bearskin shakos, George Marshall knew he wanted to join the Governor's Footguard.

George: *"I used to come down and watch on Powder House Day. I didn't know what was going on, but I knew that it was an honorable organization and that I had to be part of it one day."*

From the child who watched in wonder, George Marshall grew into a man who now helps re-create that historic day each year in New Haven with the Second

Company Governor's Footguard, one of the oldest military organizations in continuous service in the United States. (Its counterpart in Hartford, the First Company Governor's Footguard, founded in 1771, claims to be the oldest.)

The Second Company met for the first time in New Haven in December 1774. Some of the names of those who gathered at Beer's Tavern would later become well known, and their deeds would resonate through Colonial history. Among them that evening was Aaron Burr, who became vice president under Thomas Jefferson. Ethan Allen and his brother, Ira, came down from Litchfield. Allen would later lead the force that captured Fort Ticonderoga. James Hillhouse, who would be elected a U.S. senator from Connecticut was there. So was Benedict Arnold, who became a major general in the Continental Army and would eventually betray the American cause.

Barbara Bayers is a music teacher and part-time church organist from Darien. As a corporal in B Company of the Footguard, she is mindful of its history.

Barbara: *"It's awesome in the true sense of the word—awesome to know that I am perpetuating history that started in such a long line before me and will be continuing on in a long line after me. I'm just a little piece of the present. To know that it has carried on before and will carry on after me, that's a gift."*

It was April 21, 1775, when news of the Battle of Lexington reached New Haven. The guard voted to march to Cambridge to assist their fellow patriots in Massachusetts in the fight against England. The next day their commander, Benedict Arnold, assembled his men on the green. They marched to Beer's Tavern, confronted New Haven's selectmen, and demanded the key to the King's powder house so that they could arm themselves.

Two hundred twenty-five years later, on a breezy Saturday morning, the Footguard mustered on the New Haven Green to commemorate and reenact the events of the first Powder House Day.

Captain Gary Stegina played the role of Colonial Lieutenant Jesse Leavenworth.

Lieutenant Leavenworth: *"Captain Arnold, the selectmen refuse to give us any powder. They say there is not enough to defend the colony, and further they ask, why this great haste? Would we not be better off waiting 'til we have further reports from our sister colonies before proceeding?"*

Captain Benedict Arnold (played by Major Peter Wasilewski): *"Leavenworth, you will say to the selectmen that I have received their message, and unless they deliver*

me the keys to the powder house in five minutes, I will order my men to break it open and supply themselves."

Huzzahs are heard from the gathered troops.

Captain Arnold: *"Massachusetts has sent for assistance. None but God Almighty shall stop me from going today."*

Modern-day Mayor John DeStefano, in the role of a Colonial selectman, responds to Arnold.

Selectman: *"Captain Arnold, we believe you are acting hastily, but I will give you the key!"*

The events of Powder House Day have been replayed in New Haven yearly since 1904, but the Footguard emphasizes that it is not a group of reenactors but an integral part of Connecticut's militia, ready to serve the Governor and the State. The Footguard is an attached unit of the Connecticut National Guard, under the command of Brigadier General George Demers.

General Demers: *"I command the Air National Guard, which is prepared to go* into the twenty-first century. As an additional duty I am in charge of the militia units. I have the best of both worlds: the modern world with its airplanes, and the tradition and the heritage that has made this country so strong."

The Footguard has escorted every Connecticut governor since 1775 and has acted as an honor guard to fourteen presidents, including John F. Kennedy when he received an honorary degree at Yale. Throughout the year the guard marches in parades and other functions, resplendent in uniforms based on those worn by the Coldstream Guards in 1775. The uniform is now known as "Dress Winter Reds" and consists of a scarlet coat with blue facing, silver braid, and silver buttons that ends in a tail just below the back of the knees.

The coat is worn with a white vest, white knee breeches, black leggings, and a tall bearskin shako.

During their 225-year history, interest in the Guard has waned at times. But the recent recruitment of women has helped revitalize its spirit.

General Demers describes all the volunteers as the most dedicated of the forces he commands.

*M*ORE:

The First and Second Company Horse Guards complement The Governor's Footguard First and Second Companies. They are among the oldest cavalry units in existence today. Members have served in many of the country's military conflicts, including the Civil War. Connecticut citizens donate the horses. The Guards' weekly mounted military drills are open to the public. ■

General Demers: "Actually, I think they're more committed because they do this daily from their hearts. There is no compensation; they do it out of patriotism. They want to make sure that the Footguard's history is not forgotten."

The Governor's Footguard, safeguarding a long and proud history that is positively Connecticut. ■

ABOUT THE AUTHOR

Diane Smith is co-host of the Morning Show with Ray Dunaway on WTIC-AM News Talk 1080. She produces programs for Connecticut Public Television based on her popular series *Positively Connecticut,* and she is the author of the book by the same name.

Diane was a news anchor and reporter at WTNH News Channel 8 in New Haven, Connecticut, for more than sixteen years, where her reporting earned her an Emmy Award. Her public affairs documentaries have earned state and national awards from the Associated Press, the Society of Professional Journalists, the National Commission against Drunk Driving, and other organizations.

She was awarded the Connecticut Tourism Industry's 1999 Media Award for *Positively Connecticut.* The American Cancer Society honored her for her work in educating women about breast cancer, and Domestic Violence Services of Greater New Haven gave Diane its Sofie Turner Award in March 2000 for her statewide work in promoting efforts to reduce domestic violence. Her extensive community service also includes work for Easter Seals, Leave a Legacy, IMPAC-CT State University Award for Young Writers, and The Women's Campaign School at Yale University.

Born in Newark, New Jersey, and a graduate of the State University of New York at Binghamton, Diane lives on the Connecticut shoreline with her husband, Tom Woodruff, and her dogs Chancellor and Chester. She encourages readers to visit her Web site at www.positivelyct.com.